1 5400 00151 3759

D0828520

Echoes of the Marseillaise

Echoes of the Marseillaise

Two Centuries Look Back on the French Revolution

E. J. Hobsbawm

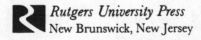
Rutgers University Press
New Brunswick, New Jersey

FEB 17 1997

DOUGLAS COLLEGE LIBRARIES

Copyright © 1990 by E.J. Hobsbawm
All rights reserved
Manufactured in Finland by Werner Söderström Oy

Library of Congress Cataloging-in-Publication Data
Hobsbawm, E.J. (Eric J.), 1917–
    Echoes of the Marseillaise: two centuries look back on the French
Revolution / Eric Hobsbawm.
       p.   cm. — (Mason Welch Gross lecture series)
    Includes bibliographical references.
    ISBN 0-8135-1523-8 (cloth) — ISBN 0-8135-1524-6 (pbk.)
    1. France—History—Revolution, 1789–1799—
Influence.   2. France—History—Revolution, 1789–1799—
Historiography.   I. Title.
    II. Series.
    DC148.H56   1990
    944.04′072—dc20

Contents

Acknowledgements

This book is a somewhat enlarged version of the three Mason Welch Gross Lectures that I was invited to give at Rutgers University, New Brunswick, New Jersey, April 1989. My first debt is, therefore, to that university for its invitation; to Rutgers University Press, which suggested publication; and, perhaps most of all, to the late Richard Schlatter, a distinguished historian and friend who initiated the invitation. Most of the writing of the lectures and their subsequent elaboration was done, under conditions of almost utopian perfection, at the J. Paul Getty Center for the History of Art and the Humanities at Santa Monica, California, where I was Visiting Scholar in the spring of 1989. My gratitude to that institution and to the colleagues and friends who were there during those months, is considerable. Ferenc Féher gave me occasion to make a preliminary exploration of some of the themes here considered, by asking me to contribute to the special issue on the French Revolution of *Social Research*, the journal of the New School for Social Research (56 no 1 [Spring 1989]), whose students have patiently listened to my lectures on "Revolution in History". One of them, Fred Longenecker, helped with the exploration of nineteenth- and early twentieth-

Acknowledgments

century periodicals. A reading of recent French commentaries on the Revolution provided the adrenalin.

Permission to reprint passages from Gramsci's *Prison Notebooks* was given by Quintin Hoare, and Geoffrey Nowell Smith and the publishers Lawrence and Wishart.

E.J.H.

Preface

In January 1989 over one thousand titles in French were available in bookshop catalogues, ready for the revolutionary bicentenary. The number published since then, and that available in other languages, of which English is by far the most important, must run into several hundreds. Is it worth adding to their number? The present essay has the excuse that it is based on the Mason Welch Gross Lectures at Rutgers, the State University of New Jersey, in 1989, and the French Revolution was an obvious subject in its bicentenary year. However, to explain is not to justify. I have two justifications.

The first is that the new literature on the French Revolution, especially in its own country, is quite extraordinarily skewed. The combination of ideology, fashion, and the power of modern media publicity has allowed the bicentenary to be largely dominated by those who, to put it simply, do not like the French Revolution and its heritage. This is not new—more was probably written against the Revolution than for it on the occasion of its first centenary—although, it is somewhat surprising to hear a (socialist) prime minister of the French Republic—Michel Rocard—welcoming the bicentenary "because it convinced a lot of people that revolution is dangerous and that if one can do without it, so much the better."[1] These are admirable sentiments that probably express a wide consensus at most times. The times when ordinary people want a revolution, let alone make one, are by definition unusual. Still, one would have thought that there are moments—1789 was one, and Monsieur Rocard could doubtless think of several others in 1989 if his mind strayed eastward from Paris, when peoples have shown signs of wanting to win Liberty, Equality, Fraternity.

The novelty about the present situation is that the memory of the Revolution is today rejected by those who dislike it on the grounds that the central tradition of French revolutionary historiography since about 1815 must be rejected as Marxist and has been shown to be unacceptable on scholarly grounds by a new school of "revisionist" historians. ("Meanwhile the tumbrils roll through the street to collect the old guard [of historians] and Marx's head is carried aloft by the mob, stuck on a pike," as a reactionary historian notes, correct in catching the mood of the times, although ignorant of the subject.)[2]

There have indeed been striking advances in research, mainly in the 1970s and mainly by British and American historians, as readers of the journal *Past and Present*, which has published articles by most of the innovating scholars, can verify.[3] However, it is wrong to suppose that this new work requires the junking of the historiography of a century, and even more mistaken to suppose that the ideological campaigns against the Revolution are based on this new research. They amount to different interpretations of what both old and new historians often accept as the same facts. Moreover, the various and sometimes conflicting "revisionist" versions of revolutionary history are not necessarily better guides to the historical role and consequences of the Revolution than older versions. Only some of the revisionists think they are. Indeed, some of the new versions are already showing signs of age, as will more in due course.

The present essay is a defence, as well as an explanation, of the older tradition. Irritation with some of its attackers is one reason for writing it. The second, and more important, reason is that it deals with a surprisingly neglected subject: the history, not of the Revolution itself, but of its reception and interpretation, its nineteenth- and twentieth-century heritage. Most specialists in the field—of whom I am not one—are too close to the events of 1789–1799, or whichever dates they choose to define the revolutionary period, to bother much about what came after. Yet the French Revolution was such an extraordinary set of events, and soon recognised universally as the foundation of the nineteenth century, that part of the history of the Revolution is what that century made of it, just as the posthumous transformation of Shakespeare into Britain's greatest literary genius, is part of the history of Shakespeare. The nineteenth century studied, copied, compared itself to, or tried to avoid, bypass, repeat, or go beyond the French Revolution. Most of this short book deals with this process of assimilating its experiences and lessons, which are, of course, far from exhausted. It is a satisfactory irony of history that the very moment when French Liberals, anxious to distance themselves from a Jacobin past, were declaring that the Revolution had nothing further to say to the present, the immediate relevance of 1789 to 1989 was being observed by students in Beijing and newly elected members of the Congress in Moscow.

And yet, the student of the nineteenth-century reception and interpretation of the Revolution must be struck by the conflict between the consensus of that century and at least some of the modern revisionist research. Even if we allow for the political and ideological bias of historians, or for the plain ignorance and lack of imagination, this needs to be explained. Revisionists tend to suggest that the Revolution really did not make all that much of a difference in French history, and that it certainly was not a change for the better. Indeed, it was "unnecessary," not in the sense that it was avoidable, but that it achieved modest—even negative—results at disproportionate costs. Few nineteenth-century observers and even fewer historians would have understood, let alone accepted, this contention. How are we to explain that intelligent and informed men of the mid nineteenth century—a Cobden, or the historian Sybel—took it for granted that the Revolution had dramatically increased French economic growth and created a massive and contented body of peasant proprietors?[4] One would not get this impression from much current research. And, although the impressions of contemporaries in themselves have no authority, and may be invalidated by serious modern research, neither are they to be dismissed as mere illusion or error. It is quite easy to show that, as economic depressions are measured today, the decades from the middle 1870s to the early 1890s were in no sense an era of secular slump, let alone a "Great Depression," yet we must still explain why otherwise sensible people with sound senses of economic reality, insisted that they were. How, then, can we explain the divergence, sometimes very wide, between old and new views?

An example may help to explain how this may come about. It has become unfashionable among economic historians today to think of the British economy, let alone any other economy, as having undergone an "industrial revolution" between 1780 and 1840, not so much for the ideological reasons that made the great biometrician Karl Pearson reject discontinuity because "no great social reconstruction, which will permanently benefit any class of the community, is ever brought about by a revolution," but because the changes in the rate of economic growth and the transformation of the economy that took place, or even its sheer quantitative increase, simply do not seem large or sudden enough in our eyes to warrant such a description. In fact, it is easy to show that, in the terms of the debates among quantitative historians, this was no "revolution."

How, then, can we explain that the term *industrial revolution* entered the vocabulary in both Britain and France in the

1820s, together with the newly devised vocabulary for the novel concept *industry*, so that by the end of the 1830s the term was already "something of a term of current use needing no explanation" among writers on social problems?[5] Moreover, it is clear that intelligent and informed people, among them men with much practical experience in technology and manufactures, predicted (with hope, fear, or satisfaction) the total transformation of society by means of industry: the Tory Robert Southey and the Socialist manufacturer Robert Owen even before Waterloo; Karl Marx and his bête noire, Doctor Andrew Ure; Frederick Engels and the scientist Charles Babbage. It seems clear that these contemporary observers were not merely paying tribute to the dramatic novelty of steam engines and the factory system, or reflecting the high social visibility of places like Manchester or Merthyr, attested to by relays of continental visitors, but were struck, above all, by the unlimited *potential* of the revolution they embodied, and the *speed* of the transformation they correctly predicted. In short, both the sceptical historians and the prophetic contemporaries were right yet each group concentrated on a different aspect of reality. One stresses the distance between 1830 and the 1980s, while the other emphasises what it saw as new and dynamic rather than what it saw as relics of the past due to move to the margins of history sooner or later.

There is a similar difference between contemporary observers and post-Napoleonic commentators on the French Revolution, as well as between historians who continued in their tracks, and the current revisionists. The question remains: which of them is more useful to the historian of the nineteenth century? Here there can be little doubt. Suppose we wish to explain why Marx and Engels wrote a *Communist Manifesto* predicting the overthrow of bourgeois society by a revolution of the proletariat, child of the industrial revolution in 1847; why the "spectre of communism" haunted so many observers in the 1840s; why representatives of the revolutionary workers were included in the French Provisional Government after the

1848 Revolution, and politicians briefly considered whether the flag for the new republic should be red or tricoloured. The history that merely tells us how far the reality of western Europe was from its image in radical circles, is of little use. It merely tells us the obvious, namely that capitalism in 1848, so far from being on its last legs, was barely getting into its stride—as indeed even social revolutionaries were soon to recognise. What does need explaining is why, in spite of the quantitatively feeble development of industrial capitalism, the idea that politics in France, and perhaps everywhere, turned on a class struggle between bourgeois entrepreneurs and wageworkers, or that communism itself could regard itself, and be feared, as a threat to bourgeois society, could have been taken seriously by anyone. Yet it was, and not only by a few young hotheads.

A historical interpretation rooted in the contemporary context—intellectual as well as social and political; existential as well as analytical— is indispensable to historians who want to answer questions about the past. Perhaps even about the present. It may or may not be correct to demonstrate, by archive and equation, that nothing very much changed between the 1780s and the 1830s, but until we understand that people saw themselves as having lived through, and as living through, an era of revolution—a process of transformation that had already convulsed the continent and would go on convulsing it—we shall understand nothing about the history of the world after 1789. All of us inevitably write out of the history of our own times when we look at the past and, to some extent, fight the battles of today in period costume. But those who write *only* out of the history of their own times, cannot understand the past and what came out of it. They may even, without intending to, falsify both past and present.

This work has been written in the belief that the two hundred years since 1789 cannot be overlooked if we want to understand "the most terrible and momentous series of events in all history.... the real starting-point for the history of the nineteenth century," as the British historian J. Holland Rose called it. And, although I share the view that the effect of that Revolution on humanity and its history has been beneficent, in the belief that political judgement is less important than analysis. After all, as the great Danish literary critic, Georg Brandes, said à propos of Hippolyte Taine's impassioned attack on the Revolution in his *Origins of Contemporary France*, what is the point of preaching a sermon against an earthquake? (Or in favour of it?)

E. J. Hobsbawm
Santa Monica and London, 1989

====== 1 ======

A Revolution of the Middle Class

The subtitle of this book is "Two Centuries Look Back on the French Revolution." Looking backward, forward, or in any direction, always implies a point of view—in time, space, mental attitude, or other subjective perspective. What I see from my window overlooking Santa Monica as I write this, is real enough. I am not inventing the buildings, the palm trees, the parking lot six floors below me, or the hills beyond, barely visible through the smog. To this extent the theorists who see all reality purely as a mental construction beyond which analysis cannot penetrate, are mistaken, and in saying so at the outset, I am nailing my conceptual colours to some kind of mast. If the history we write about were indistinguishable from fiction, there would be no room for the profession of historian, and people like me would have been wasting their lives. Nevertheless, it is undeniable that what I see out of my window, or in looking back at the past, is not only the reality out there or back there, but a highly specific selection. It is both what I *can* see physically from the point where I find myself and under the given circumstances—for instance I cannot, without going to the other side of the building, see in the direction of Los Angeles, and I cannot see much of the

1

hills until the weather improves—and what I am *interested* in seeing. Out of the infinity of what is objectively observable out there, I am in fact observing only a very limited selection. And, of course, if I were to look out at exactly the same scene from the same window some other time, I might find myself focusing on different aspects of it; that is, making a different selection. Nevertheless, it is almost inconceivable that I, or anyone else, looking out of this window at *any* time while the view remains as it is, would not see, or more precisely notice, certain inescapable features of the landscape: for instance the slim church spire just to one side of the large flat slab of an eighteen-storey building, and the cubic tower on top of its flat roof.

I do not want to labour this analogy between looking at a landscape and looking at a part of the past. In any case, I shall be returning to the point I have tried to make in the course of these pages. As we shall see, what people have read into the French Revolution as they have looked back on it in the two hundred years since 1789 has varied enormously, largely for political and ideological reasons. Yet two things about it have been generally accepted. The first is the general shape of the landscape at which they looked. Whatever the theories about the origins of the Revolution, all agree that there was a crisis in the old monarchy which, in 1788, led to the calling of the States General—the assembly representing the three estates of the realm, clergy, nobility, and the rest, the "Third Estate"— for the first time since 1614. Since they were first established the main political landmarks remain unchanged: the transformation of the States General, or rather the Third Estate, into the National Assembly, the acts visibly ending the old regime—the taking of the Bastille, the royal prison, on 14 July; the giving up of their feudal rights by the nobility on 4 August 1789; the Declaration of Rights; the transformation of the National Assembly into a Constituent Assembly that, between 1789 and 1791, revolutionised the administrative structure and organisation of the country, incidentally introducing the metric system to the world, and that drafted the first of the nearly twenty constitutions of modern France, a liberal constitutional monarchy. There is equally no disagreement about the facts of the double radicalisation of the Revolution after 1791, which led, in 1792, to the outbreak of war between revolutionary France and a varying coalition of counterrevolutionary foreign powers and domestic counterrevolutionary insurrections. This lasted, almost without a break, until 1815. It also led to the second Revolution of August 1792, which abolished the monarchy and instituted the Republic—a new, utterly revolutionary era in human history—symbolised, with a slight delay, by a new calendar. Starting at year I, the calendar abolished the ancient weekly division, giving the months new names in order to provide history students with headaches but also with useful mnemonics. (The new era and its calendar lasted just twelve years.)

The period of the radical revolution from 1792 to 1794, and especially the period of the Jacobin Republic, also known as "The Terror" of 1793–1794, form an even more universally recognised landmark; as does the end of the Terror, the famous Ninth Thermidor, which saw the arrest and execution of its leader Robespierre—although, about no period of the Revolution have opinions differed more dramatically. The regime of moderate liberalism and graft that took over for the next five years lacked an adequate basis of political support or the ability to restore conditions of stability and, as once again everyone agrees, it was replaced on the famous Eighteenth Brumaire in 1799 by a barely disguised military dictatorship, the first of many in modern history, and as a result of the coup of a successful young ex-radical general, Napoleon Bonaparte. Most modern historians end the French Revolution at this point, although, as we shall see, during the first half of the nineteenth century, the regime of Napoleon, at all events until he declared himself Emperor in 1804, was very commonly seen as the institutionalisation of the new revolutionary society. You may recall that Beethoven did not withdraw the dedication of the Eroica symphony to Napoleon until after he had ceased to be the head of a Republic. The basic succession of events, the Revolution's nature and periodisation, are not in dispute. Whatever our disagreements about the Revolution, and about its landmarks, insofar as we see the same landmarks in its historical landscape, we are talking about the same thing. (This is not always the case in history.) Mention the Ninth Thermidor and everyone who takes the slightest interest in the French Revolution knows what we mean: the fall and execution of Robespierre, the end of the most radical phase of the Revolution.

The second notion about the Revolution that was universally accepted, at all events until very recently, is in some ways more important: that the Revolution was an episode of profound, unparalleled significance in the history of the entire modern world, whatever exactly we believe that significance to have been. It was, to return to the quotation from Holland Rose "the most terrible and momentous series of events in all history.... the real starting-point for the history of the nineteenth century; for that great upheaval has profoundly affected the political and, still more, the social life of the Continent of Europe."[1] There was, thought a German liberal historian of 1848—Karl von Rotteck—"no greater event in world history than the French Revolution, indeed hardly any event of equal greatness."[2] Other historians were less extreme, they merely thought it was the most important historical event since the fall of the Roman Empire in the fifth century A.D. Some of the more Christian or, among the Germans, more patriotic, were prepared to think of the Crusades and the (German) Reformation, as comparable, but Rotteck, who considered such alternative candidates as the foundation of Islam, the reforms of the medieval Papacy and the Crusades, dismissed them. To him, the only developments that had changed the world to the same extent were Christianity and the invention of writing and of print—and all of these changed the world only *gradually*. But the French Revolution "abruptly and with irresistible

4

force, convulsed the continent that gave it birth. It also hurled its thunderbolts on the other continents. Since it emerged it has been virtually the only object to be considered on the scene of world history."[3]

Let us, therefore, take it for granted that people in the nineteenth century, or at least the literate section of them, regarded the French Revolution as supremely important; as an event or a series of events of unprecedented size, scale, and impact. This was due not only to the enormous historical consequences that seemed obvious to observers, but also to the peculiarly dramatic and spectacular nature of what had taken place in France and, through France in Europe and even beyond, in the years after 1789. The Revolution, thought Thomas Carlyle, who wrote an early, impassioned, and highly coloured history of it in the 1830s, was in some sense not only a European revolution—he saw it as the predecessor of Chartism—but the great *poem* of the nineteenth century; a real-life equivalent to the myths and epics of ancient Greece, yet written not by a Sophocles or a Homer, but by life itself.[4] It was a history of terror—and indeed the period of the Jacobin Republic of 1793–1794 is still commonly known as The Terror, even though, by our standards of massacre, it killed only modest numbers: perhaps a few tens of thousands. In Britain, for instance, this was the image of the Revolution that came closest to entering public consciousness, thanks to Carlyle and Dickens's (Carlyle-inspired) *A Tale of Two Cities*, followed by pop-literary epigones like Baroness Orczy's *The Scarlet Pimpernel*: the knock of the guillotine's blades, the sansculotte women knitting impassively as they watched the counterrevolutionary heads fall. Simon Schama's *Citizens*, the 1989 bestseller written for the English-language market by an expatriate British historian, suggests that this popular image is still very much alive. It was a history of heroism and of great deeds, of ragged soldiers led by generals in their twenties conquering all Europe, and plunging the continent and the seas into almost a quarter-century of virtually continuous war.

It produced larger-than-life heroes and villains: Robespierre, Saint-Just, Danton, Napoleon. For intellectuals it produced prose of marvellous laconic lucidity and force. In short, whatever else the Revolution was, it was a superspectacle.

Yet the major impact of the Revolution on those who looked back on it in the nineteenth, and indeed in the twentieth century was not literary but political, or more generally, ideological. In this book I shall consider three aspects of this retrospective analysis. First, I shall look at the French Revolution as a bourgeois revolution, and indeed as, in some sense, the prototype of bourgeois revolutions. Next, I shall look at it as a model for subsequent revolutions, especially social revolutions or those who wanted to make them. And finally, I shall consider the shifting political attitudes reflected in the commemorations of the French Revolution between its first and its second centenaries and their impact on those who wrote and continue to write its history.

It is today not merely unfashionable to see the French Revolution as a "bourgeois revolution," but many excellent historians would regard this interpretation of the Revolution as exploded and untenable. So, although I shall have no difficulty in showing that the earliest serious students of the history of the Revolution—incidentally men who had actually lived through the years from 1789 to 1815—saw it in precisely this manner, I shall have to say a preliminary word about the current phase of historical revisionism about the Revolution, which was initiated by the late Alfred Cobban of London University in the middle 1950s. This became a massive onslaught in 1970 when François Furet and Denis Richet criticised the established view of revolutionary history, as taught from the Sorbonne chair (established for this purpose almost a century earlier).[5] In the final chapter, I shall return to the canonical succession of professors who defended the Revolution and the Republic. Here it is relevant to observe only that the revisionist attack was directed primarily against what was seen as a—or rather *the*—Marxist interpretation of the Revolution as formulated in the twenty years or so before and after World War II. Whether this was or was not Marx's own interpretation is a relatively trivial question, especially because the fullest scholarly survey of Marx and Engels's views on the subject shows that their opinions on it, never systematically expounded, were sometimes inconsistent or incoherent. It is, however, worth mentioning in passing that, according to the same scholars, the concept of a bourgeois revolution (*bürgerliche* revolution) occurs no more than about a dozen times in the thirty-eight massive volumes of the two authors' *Werke.*[6]

The view that has been controverted is the one that sees the French eighteenth century as a class struggle between a rising capitalist bourgeoisie and an established ruling class of feudal aristocrats, which the rising bourgeoisie, conscious of itself as a class, fought to replace as the dominant force in society. This view saw the Revolution as the triumph of that class and, consequently, as the historical mechanism for ending feudal–aristocratic society and inaugurating nineteenth-century bourgeois capitalist society, which, it was implied, could not otherwise have broken through what Marx, speaking of the proletarian revolution he saw as destined to overthrow capitalism, called "the integument of the old society." In short, revisionism criticised (and criticises) the concept of the French Revolution as essentially a necessary social revolution, an essential and inevitable step in the historical development of modern society, and, of course, as the transfer of power from one class to another.

There is no doubt that something like this view was widely held, and not only among Marxists. However, it must also be said that the great historical specialists who operated in this tradition are far from being reducible to such a simple model. Moreover, again this model was not a specifically Marxist one, although—for reasons I shall discuss in the last chapter—between 1900 and the Second World War, the orthodox tradition of revolutionary historiography found itself converging with the Marxist tradition. It is also clear why such a model would suit Marxists. It provided, as it were, a bourgeois precedent for the coming triumph of the proletariat. The workers were another class born and grown to irresistible strength within an old society they were destined to take over. Their triumph would also and *inevitably* be achieved through revolution; and, just as bourgeois society had been in relation to the feudalism that preceded it and that it had overthrown, the new socialist society would be the next and higher phase of the development of human society. In the communist era it suited the Marxists even better, since it suggested that no other mechanism except revolution could transform society rapidly and fundamentally.

I need not summarise the arguments that have made this view untenable as a description of what took place in late eighteenth-century France. Let us merely accept that there was not, in 1789, a self-conscious bourgeois class representing the new realities of economic power, prepared to take the destinies of state and society into its own hands; and insofar as such a class can be discerned in the 1780s, its object was not to make a social revolution but rather to reform the institutions of the kingdom; and, in any case, it did not envisage the systematic construction of an industrial capitalist economy. And yet the problem of bourgeois revolution does not go away once we have shown that there were no distinct and antagonistic classes of bourgeois and nobles in 1789 fighting for supremacy. For, if I may quote Colin Lucas, whose work, "Nobles, Bourgeois and the Origins of the French Revolution," has been extensively used by French revisionists, if there were no distinct and antagonistic classes in 1789

in that case we have to decide why, in 1788–9 groups which can be identified as non-noble combatted groups which can be identified as noble, thereby laying the foundations of the political system of the nineteenth-century bourgeoisie; and why they attacked and destroyed privilege in 1789, thereby destroying the formal organization of eighteenth-century French society and thereby preparing a structure within which the socio-economic development of the nineteenth century might blossom.[7]

In other words, we have to discover why the French Revolution was a bourgeois revolution even though nobody intended it to be.

This is a problem that did not worry the men who first saw the French Revolution as a social revolution, a class struggle, and a bourgeois victory over feudalism in the years immediately following the final defeat of Napoleon. They were themselves moderate Liberals, and as like as not class-conscious *bourgeois*, give or take the odd moderate Liberal such as de Tocqueville, who belonged to the old aristocracy. In fact, as Marx himself freely acknowledged, these were the men from whom he derived the idea of the class struggle in history.[8] They were essentially historians of their own times. François Guizot was twenty-eight years old when Napoleon was sent to Saint Helena, Augustin Thierry was twenty, Adolphe Thiers and F.A. Mignet nineteen, and Victor Cousin twenty-three. Indeed, P.L. Roederer—who saw the Revolution as having been made *before* the event "dans les moeurs de la classe moyenne" ("in the ways of behaviour of the middle class"), and whose idea of the predestined secular rise of the middle classes and the replacement of land by capital was written in 1815—had been born in 1754 and had played an active part in the Revolution itself.[9] He was a little older than Antoine Barnave, a moderate who fell under the guillotine but whose "Introduction to the French Revolution," written while awaiting death, had taken a similar line. His text was used in Jean Jaurès' Socialist *History of the French Revolution* as the foundation of the socialist class interpretation. In writing about the French Revolution these men were forming a judgment on what they themselves had lived through, and certainly what parents, teachers, and friends had experienced at first hand.

And what they were patently doing when they began to write history in the early 1820s was, to cite a recent French text, "celebrating the epic of the French middle classes."[10]

That epic, for Guizot and Thierry, as for Marx, began long before the Revolution—in fact, with the winning of autonomy by medieval city burghers from feudal lords, and thus constituted itself into the nucleus of what was to become the modern middle class.

> The bourgeoisie, a new nation, whose manners and morals are constituted by civil equality and independent labour, now arose between nobles and serfs, and thus destroyed forever the original social duality of early feudalism. Its instinct for innovation, its activity, *the capital it accumulated* [emphasis added], formed a force that reacted in a thousand ways against the power of those who possessed the land.[11]

"The continuous elevation of the *tiers état* is the predominant fact and the law of our history," Thierry thought. The historical rise of this class, and its accession to power, was demonstrated and ratified by the Revolution, and even more by the Revolution of 1830, which Thierry saw as "the providential termination of all the centuries since the twelfth."[12]

François Guizot, a surprisingly interesting historian who became Prime Minister of France in the selfconsciously bourgeois regime of 1830–1848, was even more unmistakable. The aggregate of local burgher emancipations in the Middle Ages "created a new and general class." For, although there was no link between these burghers and they had no common and public existence as a class, "men engaged in the same situation throughout the country, possessing the same interests, the same way of life [*moeurs*] could not but fail gradually to engender certain mutual links, a certain unity, from which was to be born the bourgeoisie. The formation of a great social class, the bourgeoisie, was the necessary consequence of the local enfranchisement of the burghers."[13] And not only this. The emancipation of the medieval communes produced the class struggle, "that struggle which fills modern history: Modern Europe is born in the struggle of the different classes of society."[14] However, the new and gradually developing bourgeoisie was limited by what Gramsci would have called its *subalternity* and what Guizot called "the prodigious timidity of spirit of the bourgeois, their humility, the excessive modesty of the claims they made in respect of the government of their country, the ease with which they could be satisfied."[15] In short, the bourgeoisie was slow to stake its claim as a ruling class; to show what Guizot called "that truly political spirit which aspires to influence, to reform, to govern."[16] And, by implication, that was the claim it should stake out. In 1829, under the reactionary government of Charles X, which was shortly to be overthrown by a truly bourgeois revolution, it was impossible to speak out more clearly from a university platform.

But what precisely would be the character of the society ruled by the bourgeoisie once it had finally decided "to influence, to reform, to govern"? Was it, as the conventional view of the Revolution still holds and in spite of denials by the "revisionists," "the era of liberal capitalism based on private property, equality before the law and *les carrières ouvertes* (in theory at least) *aux talents*"?[17] There can be no serious doubt about the intention of the spokesmen for the *tiers état*, let alone the Restoration Liberals, to install the last three items. The *Declaration of the Rights of Man* said as much. Nor can there be much doubt about the first, even though in 1789 neither the term *liberal* nor *capitalism* existed, or had their modern connotations, nor does the term *capitalism* appear in French in anything hinting at the current meaning before the 1840s, the decade when *laissez-faire* as a noun also enters the vocabulary.[18] (However *capitalist*, in the sense of a person living off investment income, is recorded in 1798.)

For freedom of enterprise, noninterference in the affairs of the economy, were certainly what such men favoured. The very fact that the international slogan of such a policy ("laissez-

11

faire, laissez passer") is of French origin, and several decades old by 1789, would suggest as much.[19] As would the popularity and influence of Adam Smith, whose *Wealth of Nations*, by the regretful admission of the French themselves, "ruined the French economists who were the foremost in the world.... He ruled alone for the best part of a century."[20] There had been at least three French editions of his work before the Revolution, and another four were published during the revolutionary period (1790–1791, 1795, 1800–1801, 1802) (without counting the first edition of his disciple J.-B. Say's *Traité d'Economie Politique* [1803], for the author only fully came into his own with the Restoration), and there were only five further French editions of *The Wealth of Nations* from the fall of Napoleon to the end of the nineteenth century.[21] It can hardly be denied that this demonstrates considerable interest during the revolutionary period in the prophet of what would today undoubtedly be called the economics of liberal capitalism.

One cannot even deny that the bourgeois liberals of the Restoration aimed at an *industrial* capitalism, although this cannot be said of the theorists of 1789. (But then we shall look even through Adam Smith's great work in vain for any serious anticipation of the industrial revolution, which was already about to emerge in his own country.) By the end of the Napoleonic period, the connection between economic development and industrialisation were already evident. The economist J.-B. Say, himself a former associate of the Girondins, had tried his hand as a master cotton-spinner, and had been confirmed in his free-trade convictions by the obstacles he had encountered in Napoleon's policy of state interference. By 1814, Saint-Simon already saw industry (in the modern meaning of the word) and industrialists (his own coinage) as the foundation of the future, and the term *Industrial Revolution* was about to make its way into both French and German vocabularies, by analogy with the French Revolution.[22] Moreover, the link between progress, political economy, and industry was already clear in the minds of young Liberal philosophers.

Victor Cousin declared in 1828: "The mathematical and physical sciences are a conquest of the human intelligence over the secrets of nature; industry is a conquest of the freedom of volition over the forces of this same nature.... The world, such as the sciences of mathematics and physics, and, following in their train, industry, have made it, is a world like unto man, reconstructed by him in his own image."[23] "Political economy" Cousin announced—that is, Adam Smith—"explains the secret, or rather the detail, of all this; it follows the achievements of industry, which are themselves connected with those of the mathematical and physical sciences."[24] What is more

> industry will not be static and immobile, but progressive. It will not be content to receive from nature what nature is ready to grant it.... It will exert force on the earth in order to extort from it the maximum of products; and in turn it will operate on these products in order to give them the shape which best fits the ideas of the epoch. Commerce will develop on a great scale, and all the nations which will play a role in this era shall be trading nations.... It will be the era of great maritime enterprises.[25]

It does not take much effort to recognise, behind the generalities of the young lecturer's philosophical discourse, the model of nineteenth-century society in his mind: it was visible from France across the Channel. We shall return to the British orientation of French liberalism in a moment.

The point to note here is not that the idea of an *industrial* economy as such did not clearly emerge until after the Napoleonic era, as both Saint-Simon and Cousin witness, at which point the general concept seems to have been familiar on the intellectual Left, but that it emerged as the natural prolongation of eighteenth-century illuminist thinking. It was the product of the combination of the "progress of enlightenment" in general, liberty, equality, and political economy, and the material advance of production. The novelty lay in making

13

the triumph of this progress depend on the rise and triumph of a specific class, the *bourgeoisie*.

But where did the French Revolution fit into this scheme? F.A. Mignet's *Histoire de la Révolution Française* of 1824 provides an answer. The first such history to deserve the name, Mignet's work was preceded only by a similar and larger work by another man destined, like Guizot, for the highest political offices, Adolphe Thiers. In the old regime, Mignet held, men were divided into rival classes: the nobles and "the people" or Third Estate, "whose power, wealth, stability and intelligence were growing daily."[26] The Third Estate formulated the Constitution of 1791, which instituted a liberal constitutional monarchy. "This constitution," Mignet states, "was the work of the middle class; at that time the strongest; for, as everyone knows, the dominant power always seizes control of institutions." The middle class, in short, was now the dominant power or ruling class. Unfortunately, caught between the king and the counterrevolutionary aristocracy on one side and "the multitude" on the other, the middle class was "attacked by the one and invaded by the other."[27] If the achievements of the liberal revolution were to be maintained, civil war and foreign intervention required the mobilisation of the common people. But because the multitude was needed to defend the country, "it demanded to govern the country; so it made its own revolution, just as the middle class had done." Popular power did not last. Yet the aim of the liberal revolution was achieved, despite "anarchy and despotism; the old society was destroyed during the Revolution, and the new one established under the Empire."[28] Logically enough, Mignet ended his history of the Revolution with the fall of Napoleon in 1814.

The Revolution was therefore seen as a complex and by no means unilinear process that, nevertheless, brought to a climax the long rise of the middle class and replaced the old society by a new one. The fundamental social discontinuity it marked has rarely been expressed more elegantly and eloquently than by Alexis de Tocqueville, whose works are constantly quoted for other purposes by revisionist historians. "Our history," he wrote in his *Recollections*, "viewed from a distance and as a whole, affords, as it were, a picture of the struggle to the death between the Ancien Régime, its traditions, memories, hopes and men, as represented by the aristocracy, and the New France, led by the Middle Class."[29] Like Thierry, de Tocqueville regarded the 1830 Revolution as the second and more successful edition of 1789, made necessary by the Bourbons' attempt to turn the clock back to 1788. The 1830 Revolution, he claimed, was a triumph of the middle class "so definite and so thorough that all political power, every prerogative, and the whole government, was confined and, as it were, heaped up within the narrow limits of this one class.... Not only did it thus rule society, but it may be said to have formed it."[30] "The Revolution" as he put it elsewhere, "has entirely destroyed, or is in the process of destroying, everything in the ancient society that was derived from aristocratic and feudal institutions, everything that was in any way connected with them, everything that had the least impress of them."[31]

In the light of such assessments by men who were, after all, describing the society in which they lived, it is difficult to understand current views that the Revolution was "ineffectual in its outcome," let alone revisionist historians who hold that "in the end the Revolution benefited the same landed elite that had started it," or who see the new rising bourgeois as continuing to "s'insérer dans une volonté d'identification à l'aristocratie" ("assimilate, moved by the will to identify with the aristocracy").[32] The least one can say is that this is not how postrevolutionary France struck those who lived in it or visited it. Certainly in the view of foreign observers, as well as of Balzac, postrevolutionary France was a society in which, more than in any other, wealth was power and men were dedicated to the accumulation of it.

Lorenz von Stein, tracing the emergence of the class struggle between bourgeois and proletarians in France after the Revolution, even devised a historical explanation for this exceptional proclivity to capitalism. Under Napoleon, he argued, the crucial question of the Revolution, namely "the right of every individual to rise, by his own ability, to the highest position in civil society and state" was narrowed down to the alternative: accumulate property or make a success in the army.[33] Despotism excluded other forms of competition for public distinction. So France became rich "because, precisely through falling under despotism of the Empire, it entered the period when *wealth* constitutes *power* for each individual."[34] How we explain this notable divergence between some historians of the late twentieth century and the observers of the early nineteenth century, is another question. Whatever the answer, the fact that the moderate Liberals of the earlier period saw the consequences of the French Revolution in utterly different terms from their moderate Liberal successors in the 1980s, cannot be elided.

One thing is clear. Some time between 1814, when Mignet ended his history, and the early 1820s, the French Revolution came to be read by young middle-class Liberals, who had grown up in the 1790s and 1800s, as the culmination of the secular rise of the bourgeoisie to the position of ruling class. Note, however, that they did not identify the middle class exclusively or essentially with businessmen, even though they had little doubt that, in later terminology, bourgeois society would indeed take the form of capitalist and increasingly industrial society. Guizot, once again, expressed this with his usual lucidity. In the twelfth century, the new class consisted chiefly of merchants, small traders ("négociants faisant un petit commerce") and small proprietors of houses or land, resident in cities. Three centuries later, it also included lawyers, medical doctors, educated persons of all kinds, and all local magistrates: "The bourgeoisie took shape over time, and was formed out of varied elements. Both this chronological sequence and the diversity have usually been neglected in its history.... Perhaps the secret of its historic destiny lies precisely in the diversity of its composition at different periods of history."[35]

Sociologically, Guizot was obviously correct. Whatever the nature of the nineteenth-century middle class or bourgeoisie, it was formed by the combination of various groups situated between nobility and peasantry, who had previously seen themselves as not necessarily having much in common with each other, into a single class, conscious of itself and treated by others as such; and very notably by those whose position was based on property and those whose position was based on education (*Besitzbürgertum* and *Bildungsbürgertum*, in the revealing German terminology).[36] Nineteenth-century history is incomprehensible to anyone who supposes that only entrepreneurs were "really" bourgeois.

The bourgeois interpretation of the French Revolution became the dominant interpretation, not only among French Liberals but also among Liberals in all countries in which "commerce and liberalism," that is, bourgeois society, had not already triumphed—as, of course, Liberals believed they were destined to do everywhere. The only countries in which it had triumphed so far, Thierry thought in 1817, were France, England, and Holland. The affinity between the countries where bourgeois society had become dominant, seemed to be so close that in 1814 Saint-Simon, the prophet of industrialism, and inventor of the word, and Thierry, who was at the time his secretary, actually envisaged a single Anglo-French parliament that was to be the nucleus of a single set of all-European institutions of an all-European constitutional monarchy when the new system was universally triumphant.[37]

The Liberal historians not only saw an affinity between Britain and revolutionary France, but also saw Britain as in some ways a predecessor and model for France. Nothing is more striking, given the habitual Gallocentrism of French culture, than the concentration of these men on the history of Britain—especially Thierry and Guizot, who were both deeply influenced by Walter Scott. One might indeed say that they not only read the French Revolution as a bourgeois revolution, but the English one of the seventeenth century as well. (This is another aspect of the Restoration Liberal heritage that was to appeal to later Marxists.) There was a strong reason for this: the English precedent confirmed French middle-class Liberals, whose ideal was certainly not revolution in itself but—to quote Thierry again—"slow but uninterrupted progress", in the conviction that revolution might nevertheless be necessary, while the English example demonstrated that such a revolution could both survive the equivalent of 1793–1794 (1649 and Cromwell) or avoid it (1688) to create a system capable of progressive non-revolutionary transformation.[38]

Guizot's arguments are particularly clear, for although he insisted on the centrality of the class struggle in European history, he did not see this struggle as a zero-sum game ending in the total victory of one side and the elimination of the other, but—even in the 1820s—as generating, in the end, *within each nation* "a certain general spirit, a certain community of interests, of ideas and of sentiments which overcome diversity and warfare."[39] National unity under bourgeois hegemony appears to have been his ideal. No wonder he was fascinated by the historical development of England where, more than anywhere else in Europe, "the different elements of the social configuration [*état social*] had combined, fought and modified each other, continually obliged to compromise in common existence." Where "the civil and the religious order, aristocracy, democracy, royalty, central and local institutions, moral and political development, advanced and grew together, as it were pell-mell, not perhaps at equal speed, but never too far from each other." And England had thus been able, "more rapidly than any of the states of the continent, to reach the aim of all society, that is to say the establishment of a government both regular and free, and to develop political good sense and sound opinion on public affairs. [*Le bon sens national et l'intelligence des affaires publiques*]"[40]

There were historical reasons for this difference between

British and French evolution (this is the subject of the final lecture in Guizot's course), even though the fundamental tendency of evolution in both countries was similar. While British feudalism (the "Norman Yoke") was the conquest of a Norman nobility over an established and structured Anglo-Saxon polity, which thus allowed a structured and, as it were, institutionalised popular resistance, an appeal to former Anglo-Saxon freedoms; the French equivalent had been the conquest of the Frankish nobles over a disintegrated population of native Gauls ("nos ancêtres les Gaulois"), unreconciled but impotent. Their insurgency against the nobles in the French Revolution was thus more uncontrolled and uncontrollable, and that revolution consequently more terrible and extreme.[41] This was an attempt to explain what puzzled so many Liberal historians in the nineteenth century, namely why (in the words of Lord Acton) in France, "the passage from the feudal and aristocratic forms of society to the industrial and democratic was attended by convulsions" unlike in other nations (that is, Britain).[42] Nevertheless, the British could serve as a model for France after 1789: for if Britain had overcome its Robespierre and/or its Napoleon—Cromwell—to make possible a second, quiet and decisive revolution destined to install a permanent system—the Glorious Revolution of 1688—France could do the same. It could, and did, install the July monarchy in 1830.

Within France, therefore, the Restoration champions of bourgeois revolution were already potential moderates, seeing themselves as having already won the decisive victory of their class. Outside, it was the call for 1789 that sounded loud and clear in middle-class ears. The institutions of the Middle Ages had had their day, thought a German and suitably idealist Liberal historian. New ideas had arisen, and these had affected "above all the relations of the ranks of society [*Stände*] in human society," among which the "bourgeois rank" (*Bürgerstand*) became every day more important. And so "men began to speak and write about the Rights of Man, and to investigate the rights of those who based their claims on so-called privileges."[43] These were fighting words in the Germany of the 1830s as they no longer needed to be in France. By then the term *bourgeois*, in France, was defined by contrast with the *people (peuple)* or the *proletarians (proletaires)*, in Germany—as in the *Brockhaus* Encyclopedia of 1827—it was contrasted with *Aristocracy* on the one hand, *peasantry* on the other, the term *Bürger* itself being increasingly equated with the term *middle class* and the French *bourgeois*.[44] A bourgeois revolution was what German middle-class Liberals wanted, or felt to be necessary; and much more clearly than their French predecessors in 1788, because they had the fact and the experiences of 1789 to look back upon.

Moreover, the British parallel, which the French historians analysed a posteriori, seemed to Germans (particularly when supplemented by the earlier Revolt of the Netherlands) to set up a mechanism of historical transformation of great power and generality: "Must a great people, seeking to break through to independent political life, to freedom and power, necessarily pass through the crisis of revolution? The double example of England and France comes close to compelling us to accept this proposition." Thus wrote the German Liberal Georg Gervinus, on the eve of 1848—himself, like so many of his kind, both scholar and political activist.[45]

Like so many other ideas later taken up with enthusiasm by Marxists, this conception of the necessity of revolution, established, as it were, by historical extrapolation (what Charles de Rémusat later called "a geometrical conviction that there was a law of revolutions in the modern world"), came from the French Restoration Liberals.[46] It was also, of course, plausible, and subsequent developments have not diminished that plausibility.

At some time between the seventeenth and mid twentieth centuries, the histories of virtually all "developed" states—Sweden is among the rare exceptions—and all of the major powers of the modern world record one or more sudden discontinuities, cataclysms or historical ruptures, classifiable either as revolution or as modelled on revolution. It is too much to ascribe this simply to a combination of coincidences, although it is quite illegitimate and evidently mistaken to infer from the historical record that change by discontinuous ruptures is inevitable in all cases.

In any case, the Restoration Liberals' necessary revolution must not be confused with later versions of it. They were not concerned so much with making a case for violent overthrow of regimes or making one against gradualism. They would undoubtedly have preferred gradualism. What they needed was (a) a theory that justified the liberal revolution against the accusation that it necessarily produced Jacobinism and anarchy, and (b) a justification of the triumph of the bourgeoisie. The theory of the necessary and inevitable revolution did both, for it side-stepped criticism. Who could argue with a phenomenon beyond human volition and control, similar to a shift in the tectonic plates of the earth? For a thousand reasons, thought Victor Cousin, the revolution had been absolutely necessary, including its excesses, which were part of its "destructive mission." And for Guizot, "the shocks we call revolutions are less the symptom of what is beginning, than the declaration of what has already taken place," namely, the secular rise of the middle class.[47] Nor, indeed, did this view seem untenable to reasonable observers in the first half of the nineteenth century.

In turn, faced with the necessity of making such a bourgeois revolution and conscious that the possibility of it had come to Germany from France, even German middle-class people far from extremism found it easier to overlook the violence of the Revolution than did contemporary Englishmen who (a) had no need to take France as a model of English liberalism and (b) confronted their own eruption of social forces from below. The image of the French Revolution that penetrated most deeply into British consciousness was not 1789 or 1791 but 1793–1794, "The Terror." When Carlyle wrote his History of the Revolution in 1837 he was not only paying tribute to the grandeur of the historical spectacle, but envisaging what might be a revolt of the British labouring poor. As he made clear later, his point of reference was Chartism.[48]

French Liberals, of course, were haunted by the dangers of Jacobinism. German Liberals contemplated it with surprising calm, although German Radicals, like the revolutionary boy genius Georg Büchner, faced it without blinking.[49] Friedrich List, the champion of German economic nationalism, defended the Revolution against the accusation that it was a mere eruption of brute force. It was caused by "the awakening of the human spirit."[50] "Only what is feeble and impotent is born without pains," another Liberal German student of the French Revolution was to put it,[51] before marrying a soubrette and taking the chair of economics at the University of Prague.[52]

Yet, if it is undeniable that the immediately postrevolutionary generation of French Liberals saw the Revolution as bourgeois, it is equally clear that the class and class-struggle analysis they exemplify would have surprised all observers and participants in 1789; even those members of the Third Estate most resentful of aristocratic privilege, such as Barnave or, let us say, Figaro in Beaumarchais's play and Mozart/Da Ponte's opera. It was the Revolution itself that created the consciousness of the strata between aristocracy and the people as a *middle class* or *classe moyenne*, a term that was, in fact, to be more commonly used (except in the context of its historical development) than *bourgeoisie*, especially during the July monarchy.[53]

It was a middle class in two senses. In the first place, the Third Estate, which declared itself to be "the nation" in 1789, was, speaking operationally, not the nation itself but what the Abbé Siéyès, its most eloquent spokesman and, incidentally, a champion of Adam Smith, called "the available classes" of that Estate; namely, in the words of Colin Lucas, "the solid, unified group of professional men," the middle rank of society, who were the ones elected as its representatives. That they also saw themselves, quite sincerely, as representing the interests of the entire nation, indeed of humanity in general, because they stood for a system not founded on interest and privilege or "on prejudices and customs, but on that which is of all times and all places, on that which ought to be the ground of every constitution, the freedom and happiness of the people" cannot prevent us from observing that they were drawn from a specific social zone of the French people, and were conscious of the fact.[54] For if, in Mignet's words, the electorate of 1791— the Liberals' own revolution—was "restricted to the enlightened" who thereby "controlled all the force and power in the state," being "at the time alone qualified to control them because they alone had the intelligence necessary for the control of government" this was because they constituted an elite selected for their ability, that ability being demonstrated by economic independence and education.[55] Such an open elite, based not on birth (except inasmuch as the physical and psychological constitutions of women were believed to debar that sex from such abilities) but on talent, was inevitably composed largely of the middle ranks of society (since the nobility was not numerous, and its status was by no means positively correlated with intelligence, and the multitude had neither education nor economic means). However, because careers open to talent were the essential basis of such an elite, nothing would prevent anyone who fulfilled its criteria of membership, whatever his social origin, from acceptance into it. To quote Mignet again: "Let all share in rights *when they are capable of gaining them*" (emphasis added).

In the second place, the "available classes" of the Third Estate, who thus naturally became the shapers of the new France, were in the middle in another sense. They found themselves politically and socially opposed to both the aristocracy above and the people below. The drama of the Revolution for those whom we may in retrospect call the moderate Liberals—the word itself, like their analysis of the Revolution, did not appear in France until after the fall of Napoleon[56]—

was that the support of the people was essential against aristocracy, old regime, and counterrevolution, while the people and the middle ranks had seriously conflicting interests. As A.V. Dicey, himself the least radical-minded of Liberals, put it a century later: "Reliance on the support of the Parisian mob meant connivance at outrage and crimes which made it impossible to establish free institutions in France. Repression of the Parisian mob meant reaction, and, probably enough, the restoration of despotism."[57] In other words, without the multitude, there was no new order; with it, the constant risk of social revolution, which seemed to become reality for a brief period in 1793–1794. The makers of the new regime needed protection against both the old and the new dangers. It is hardly surprising that they should learn to recognise themselves, in the course of events, and retrospectively, as a middle class and to recognise the Revolution as a class struggle against both aristocracy and the poor.

And yet, what else could they have done? The modern revisionist view that the French Revolution was in some sense "unnecessary," that is, that nineteenth-century France would have been much as it was if the Revolution had not taken place, is the kind of counterfactual proposition that is neither testable nor plausible. Even in the more restricted sense in which it is argued that "the change attributable to the Revolution ... falls far short of what could be claimed to amount to collective mobility on such a scale as to modify the social structure" and that it was not necessary to unblock capitalism in an old regime that did not offer serious obstacles to it, and if the French Revolution did anything, it was to slow down its postrevolutionary advances, it cannot possibly imply that the moderates of 1789 could have been expected to share this view, if only because it belongs to the discourse of the late twentieth century and not to that of the late eighteenth.[58]

It was quite clear, almost from the moment the States-General were assembled, that the enlightened programme of reform and progress on which, in principle, all men of good

will and education agreed, noble or otherwise, would not be
carried out as a reform from above by the monarchy—as they
had all hoped—but by a new regime. It was carried out by a
revolution—that is, a revolution from below, since the revolution from above, however desirable in theory, was plainly no
longer an option in 1789, if it had ever been one. Indeed, it
would not have been made but for the intervention of the
common people. Nor did de Tocqueville, who reflected how
agreeable it would have been if an enlightened autocrat had
made such a revolution, suppose for a moment that this was
possible.[59] And, although at every phase of the revolutionary
process there were some who decided that matters had gone
far enough and would have preferred to call a halt, the
Restoration Liberal historians, unlike modern Liberals and
some revisionist scholars, having lived through a great revolution at first hand, knew that such events cannot be switched on
and off like television programmes. The image behind François Furet's metaphor of "skidding off course" (*dérapage*) is
unhistorical, since it implies that control of the vehicle is
possible: but getting out of control is an integral part of great
revolutions as of great twentieth-century wars or other
comparable phenomena. "Men forgot their real interests, their
concrete interests" wrote Thierry about the Revolution in
1817, "But it would have been futile to try to point out to us
the vanity of the objects we were pursuing; ... history was
there, and we could have it speak for us and confound
reason."[60] Mignet knew this better than some of his descendants in the family of moderate liberalism:

> Perhaps it would be bold to assert that things could not have
> turned out differently; but what is certain is that, taking
> account of the causes that led to it and the passions that it used
> and aroused, the revolution was bound to take this course and
> lead to this result.... It was no longer possible either to
> prevent it *or to guide it* [emphasis added].[61]

25

In Chapter 2, I shall return to the discovery of revolution as a sort of natural phenomenon escaping from human control, one of the most characteristic and important conclusions that observers drew from the experience of the French Revolution.

Nevertheless, might we not have expected the moderate Liberals of the Restoration, like their current successors, to have regretted the uncontrollable cataclysm through which France had passed, for that very reason? If the revisionists are right in regarding the quarter-century of revolution as "une péripétie cruelle" in French history, after which things went back to their slow rhythm of change, might one not have expected moderate men to reflect sometimes on the disproportionate costs of such relatively small changes?[62] Perhaps even to show some of that nostalgia for the *ancien régime*, which visitors to the parts of Europe once ruled by the Habsburg monarchy still detect among the intellectuals of countries that threw off its yoke in the days of their grandparents or great-grandparents? (Might one not, incidentally, have expected a massive reversion to monarchism among the masses whose lives had been disrupted so much and for so little?)[63] But there is no sign of such reactions.

The Restoration Liberals, however appalled by much of what had happened in their country, did not reject the Revolution and were not apologetic about it. In fact, their historiography was seen by a contemporary British Conservative as a "general conspiracy then at work against the elder Bourbons—a paradoxical apology for the old Revolution and a covert provocation to a new one."[64] The author he had in mind, Adolphe Thiers, can hardly be accused of excessive radicalism even in the 1820s.[65] Whatever the excesses of the Revolution, would not the alternative—no revolution—have been worse? As François-Xavier Joseph Droz, who had lived through The Terror as a young man, put it: "Let us not imitate those ancients who, terrified by the burning of Phaeton's chariot, asked the Gods to leave them in permanent darkness."[66]

Nothing is more striking about the Restoration Liberals than their refusal to abandon even that part of the Revolution that was indefensible in Liberal terms, which Liberals did not wish to defend, and which indeed the moderates had overthrown: the Jacobinism of 1793–1794. The Revolution they wished to preserve was that of 1789, that Declaration of the Rights of Man whose essential liberalism Tocqueville never ceased to stress or, more concretely, of the principles of the 1791 Constitution.[67] Yet was it not Guizot himself who defended the Revolution as a whole as "the necessary development of a society in progress, ... the *terrible* but *legitimate* battle of right against privilege"? Was it not Guizot who did not

> wish to disown anything of the Revolution. I do not claim to discharge it of anything. I seize it as a whole, its truths and its errors, its virtues and its excesses, its triumphs and its reverses.... You will tell me that it violated justice, oppressed liberty. I will agree with you. I will even join in examining the causes of these lamentable digressions. I will go further: I will grant you that the germ of these crimes was present in the very cradle of the Revolution.[68]

Unlike so many of those who prepared, or hesitated to prepare, the celebrations of the Revolution's bicentenary, the Restoration Liberals, with all their moderation, took the view that, "taken all in all, crimes included, the Revolution was worth having."[69]

One reason for this willingness to accept what Thierry, speaking of the English Revolution, called "necessary acts of violence," was, no doubt, that the Jacobin Terror had been a short-lived episode; moreover, an episode brought to an end by the Revolution itself. The moderates had only temporarily lost control. But another and more powerful reason was that revolution still seemed indispensable. For, just as the old regime would not have been overthrown without it in 1789, so the attempt to restore it, which they believed to be in progress, would also have to be defeated by a revolution. Behind the development of the bourgeois model of the French Revolution, which I have traced during the Restoration, there lay precisely the political struggle of moderate bourgeois Liberals against the reactionary attempt to turn back the clock. This became obvious to them in 1820, when Liberal political activists—including all the men we have been discussing—had to retreat from action into thinking and writing. "Write books" the Liberal leader Royer-Collard is supposed to have told these young intellectuals after the fall of the Decazes ministry; "there's nothing else to be done just now."[70] That is how the Restoration historical school of Guizot, Thiers, Mignet, and the rest came into being, although, when action once again became feasible, some preferred to remain in their studies. What the young historians were engaged in was the elaboration of a theory for making a bourgeois revolution. In 1830 they put it into practice.

At this point a clarification is in order. It should be clearly understood that for moderate Liberals, as distinct from the heirs of the Jacobins, the Restoration of 1814 was not an unhappy concession to reaction under the pressure of defeat, but was exactly what they wanted. Although initially uncertain, the Liberals soon saw—or found it convenient to see— Louis XVIII as a constitutional monarch, even though monarchical and international face was saved by calling the Constitution a Charter freely granted from above.[71] Napoleon had safeguarded the bourgeoisie against both the dangers that threatened it, but at a price: exclusion from politics and the absence of civic rights. The bourgeoisie had no share in power. "There were indeed rich and poor" as Lorenz von Stein put it, "but there was no ruling class and no class that was being ruled. There were only subjects."[72] But the Restoration of 1814 restored not only the monarchy, but the element of representative constitutional government that seemed so essential, and it did so without the danger of excessive democracy. It looked like institutionalising the achievements of the moderate—pre-1791—Revolution without the need for further revolution. As

Guizot put it: "revolution and legitimacy today have in common the fact that both are seeking to preserve themselves and to preserve the *status quo.*"[73] In doing so they established that "frank cooperation" by means of which "kings and nations"—Guizot was, as usual, thinking of England—"have extinguished those internal wars which are denominated revolutions." What Guizot blamed the reactionaries for was not so much the intention to restore an old regime that was beyond effective revival, but for risking the return of the masses into a perhaps necessary but always dangerous and unpredictable action. The bourgeoisie liked Louis XVIII because "for the house of Bourbon and its supporters absolute power is [now] impossible; under them France must be free."[74] In short, it was a better and more desirable safeguard than Napoleon against both the old regime and democracy. And the regime of 1830, that revolution which was actually made as a bourgeois revolution and instituted a self-consciously and class-consciously bourgeois regime, with a king who wore a top hat instead of a crown, was an even more desirable solution. It even seemed to have solved the crucial problem of moderate bourgeois liberalism, namely how to control the revolutionary mobilisation of the masses. As it turned out, it had not.

Indeed, the Revolution was necessarily *both* 1789 and 1793–1794, both moderate and Jacobin. Every attempt to separate one from the other, to accept Mirabeau but reject Robespierre, is unrealistic. This does not of course mean identifying the two, as nineteenth-century conservatives were apt to do: "Jacobinism, now called by the new name of Liberalism" as the Dutch protestant ideologist Isaac Da Costa (1798–1860) wrote in 1823.[75] The ideologists of bourgeois liberalism tried hard to keep democracy at bay—that is, the intervention of the poor and labouring majority. The Restoration Liberals and the 1830 Constitution did so more ruthlessly than the Constitution of 1791, since they looked back on the experience of Jacobinism. They believed, as we have seen in Mignet's

29

electorate "restricted to the enlightened," who "controlled all the force and power in the state," because they were alone qualified to control it. They believed not in equal rights for all citizens but that for them the real hallmark of "true equality," to quote Mignet again, was "admissibility" just as the hallmark of inequality was "exclusion."[76] Liberal democracy seemed to them a contradiction in terms: either liberalism, which was based on a meritocratic elite with open entry, or democracy. The experience of the Revolution had even made them suspicious of a Republic, which, in France, was linked to Jacobinism. What would really have suited them was something like the constitutional monarchy of Whig Britain—perhaps something a little more logical and systematic and less haphazard, preferably introduced by a controlled revolution like 1688. In 1830 they thought they had found it.

But it would not work. There was no way of stopping on the road, once the gate of 1789 had been passed. Here lies the enormous merit of de Tocqueville, a Liberal of aristocratic origins, who did not quite share the illusions of a Guizot or a Thiers. De Tocqueville's writings on the French Revolution have been misread as a statement that it was not necessary, and in favour of the historic continuity of French evolution. But, as we have seen, nobody was more convinced that the Revolution marked a major and irreversible break with the past than he. Similarly, his writings on democracy in America have been read, especially in America, as appreciations of the merits of that system. But this is not so. De Tocqueville recognised that, as much as he and other educated men feared democracy, there was no way of preventing it in the long run. It was implicit in liberalism. But could this system be made to work without producing Jacobinism and social revolution? This was the question that led him to investigate the United States. He concluded that a non-Jacobin version of democracy was possible. However, with all his readiness to appreciate American democracy, it did not make him enthusiastic about the system. When he wrote his remarkable work, de Tocqueville probably thought, and certainly hoped, that 1830 provided a permanent framework for the further evolution of French society and institutions. He merely wished to point out, correctly, that even so it must inevitably broaden in order to operate through the political democracy that, like it or not, it generated. In the long run, bourgeois society did so, but it did not seriously try to until after 1870, even in the country of the Revolution itself. And, as we shall see in the last chapter, the assessment of the Revolution at its first centenary was to be largely dominated by this problem.

The fundamental fact remained, and still remains: 1789 and 1793 belong together. Both bourgeois liberalism and the social revolutions of the nineteenth and twentieth centuries claim the inheritance of French Revolution. In this chapter I have tried to show how the programme of bourgeois liberalism was crystallised in the experience of, and the reflection on, the French Revolution. In the next chapter we shall consider the Revolution as a model for subsequent social revolutions that set out to go beyond liberalism, and, as a point of reference, for those who observed and assessed such revolutions.

2

Beyond the Bourgeoisie

The French Revolution dominated the history, even the language, and the symbolism of western politics from its outbreak until the period following the First World War—including the politics of those elites in what is today called the Third World who saw their people's hopes in some kind of modernisation, that is, in following the example of the most advanced European states. Thus, the French tricolour flag patently provided the model for the flags of the majority of newly independent or unified states in the world for almost a century and a half: unified Germany chose black, red, and gold (and later black, white, and red) instead of blue, white, and red; unified Italy green, white, and red; and, by the 1920s, twenty-two states had adorned themselves with national flags consisting of three strips of different colours, vertical or horizontal, and another two with three-colour blocks in red, white, and blue, which also suggest French influence. By comparison, the national flags showing the direct influence of the Stars and Stripes were few indeed, even if we take a mere single star in the top lefthand corner as a sign of a United States derivation: a maximum of five, of whom three—Liberia, Panama, and Cuba—were virtually created by the United

States. Even within Latin America the flags showing tricolour influence outnumbered those showing northern influence. Indeed, the comparatively modest international influence of the American Revolution—except, of course, on the French Revolution itself—must strike the observer. As a model for changing social and political systems it was absorbed, as it were, and replaced by the French Revolution, partly because reformers or revolutionaries in European societies could recognise themselves more readily in the *ancien régime* of France than in the free colonists and slave-holders of North America. Also, the French Revolution saw itself, far more than the American had, as a global phenomenon, the model and pioneer of the world's destiny. Among the numerous revolutions of the late eighteenth century it is singled out not only by its scale, and—in terms of the state system—centrality, not to mention its drama, but also from the start, by this consciously ecumenical dimension.

For obvious reasons, those who proposed to make revolutions, and especially revolutions whose object was the fundamental transformation of the social order ("social revolutions"), were particularly inspired and influenced by the model of France. From the 1830s, or, at the latest, the 1840s, these included the new social movements of the working classes in the countries of industrialisation, or at least the organisations and movements claiming to speak on behalf of these new classes. In France itself, the ideology and language of the Revolution spread after 1830 to regions and strata that had been left untouched by it in the original revolutionary era, including large areas of the countryside. The process has been wonderfully described and analysed for parts of Provence in Maurice Agulhon's *La République au Village*.[1] Outside France, peasants, on the whole, remained hostile to ideologies brought to them by men from cities, even when they could understand them, and justified their own movements of social protest and revolt in different terminology. Governments, ruling classes, and the ideologists of the left, until well into the second half of the nineteenth century, usually agreed—with satisfaction or resignation—that peasants were conservatives. This underestimate of the radical potential of the agriculturists by the Left is very noticeable in the 1848 revolutions, and was reflected in their historiography until long after World War II, even though there are hints, in the aftermath of 1848, that Frederick Engels did not consider the second edition of the peasant war for which he called (meanwhile writing a popular history of it) totally utopian. He had, of course, seen action himself with the armed revolutionaries in Southwest Germany, part of the country where, as historians are now realising, 1848 was essentially an agrarian movement, and perhaps the largest such movement in Germany since the sixteenth-century peasant war.[2] Nevertheless, even for revolutionary peasants the French Revolution was remote. The young Georg Büchner, author of the astonishing *Danton's Death*, did not address the peasantry of his native Hesse in Jacobin language, but in the language of the Lutheran Bible.[3]

Not so for the urban or industrial workers, who found no difficulty in taking to the language and symbolism of the Jacobin revolution, that the French ultraleft had—especially after 1830—adapted specifically to their situation, identifying the people with the proletariat. The French workers in 1830 adapted the rhetoric of the Revolution for their own purposes, even though they had become conscious of themselves as a class movement *against* the Liberal authorities who also appealed to this rhetoric, and not only in France.[4] The German and Austrian socialist movements, perhaps through the identification of their leaders with the 1848 Revolution—Austrian workers celebrated the anniversary of the victims of March 1848 (*Märzgefallene*) before they celebrated the First of May—stressed their continuity with the Great Revolution. The *Marseillaise* (in various textual adaptations) was the anthem of German Social Democracy, and Austrian Social Democracy in 1890 still put the Phrygian bonnet—characteristic headgear of the Revolution—and the slogan Equality,

Liberty, Fraternity, on its May Day badges.[5] This is not surprising. After all, the ideology and language of social revolution came to central Europe from France, through radical German journeymen on their wide-ranging travels, German political emigrés or tourists in pre-1848 Paris, and through the sometimes extremely well-informed and influential publications some of them brought back, notably Lorenz (von) Stein's.[6] By the time important socialist labour movements developed in continental Europe, the tradition of the French Revolution as an active, insurrectionary, political transformation, had in fact been reduced largely to its working-class component. The Paris Commune of 1871 linked the Jacobin with the proletarian social-revolutionary tradition, not least through Karl Marx's eloquent analytical obituary of it.[7]

That the French Revolution lived on through 1793–1794, as well as through 1789, was only too evident to worried observers. For 1848, although apparently a brief episode rapidly defeated in most of the numerous countries convulsed by revolution, certainly demonstrated that the revolutionary process continued. In France the hope that it had found a firm conclusion in 1830, gave way to pessimism and uncertainty among Liberals. "I don't know when this voyage will end" exclaimed de Tocqueville in the 1850s. "I am tired of thinking, time and again, that we have reached the coast and finding it was only a misleading bank of fog. I often wonder whether that solid ground we have so long sought really exists, or whether our destiny is not rather to sail a storm-tossed sea forever."[8] Outside France, using the same simile, Jakob Burckhardt opened his course on the French Revolution in the 1870s with the words: "We know that the same storm which hit mankind in 1789 is still driving us into the future."[9]

In this situation the French Revolution came to serve a number of purposes. For those who wanted to transform society, it provided an inspiration, a rhetoric and a vocabulary, a model, and a standard of comparison. For those who did not need or want to make revolution, the first three of these uses were less important (except in France), although a major part of the political vocabulary of all western nineteenth-century states derived from the Revolution and was often directly borrowed or adapted from the French: for example most of what is associated with "the nation." On the other hand, the Revolution as a standard of comparison was, if anything, more important—for the fear of revolution is more common than the actual prospect of it. And although, as we shall see, for most of the new western—working-class and socialist—Left, the operational relevance of 1789–1799 was increasingly faint, unlike the ideological relevance, governments and ruling classes were constantly assessing the possibilities of subversion and the rebellion of men and women who, as they knew well enough, had plenty of good reasons to be discontented with their lot. Past revolutions were the obvious points of reference. Thus, in 1914 the British minister John Morley wondered if the mood of the country, on the eve of what proved to be World War I, but in the midst of considerable sociopolitical unrest, was not like that preceding 1848.[10] When a revolution actually broke out, both those who favoured and those who opposed it would immediately compare it to its predecessors. The larger and more central it was, the more inescapable the comparison with 1789.

Thus, in July 1917 the *Current History Magazine* of the *New York Times* published an anonymous article whose title, "The Russian and French Revolutions 1789–1917: Parallels and Contrasts" unquestionably reflected the preoccupations of every educated European or American at the time.[11] Probably a fair number of them would also have agreed with his not exceptionally perceptive observations. In both countries, thought the author, "had the sovereign wisely and loyally yielded at the critical moment, establishing genuine representative institutions ... no revolution would have taken place. In both countries, likewise, the final and fatal opposition came from the foreign queen (Marie Antoinette in one case, the German-born Tsarina in the other), and through her dangerous power over the sovereign." In both countries, he argued, philosophers and writers had long prepared for the revolution—Voltaire and Rousseau in one case, Tolstoi, Herzen, and Bakunin in the other. (The author of the essay did not rate Marx's influence highly.) He drew a parallel between the French Council of Notables, replaced by the Estates-General and the Constituent Assembly in one case, and the Russian Council of Empire, replaced by the Imperial Duma, in the other. Looking at the internal development of the Revolution, which of course had not progressed very far by the summer of 1917, the author saw the Liberal Kadet party, Rodsianko and Miliukov, corresponding to the Girondins, and the Soviet of Workers and Soldiers' Deputies to the Jacobins. (Insofar as this might imply that the Liberals would be overthrown by the Soviets, this was not a bad prediction, although, in other respects the author does not make a particularly acute impression.)

What these comparisons focused on was not the Liberal revolution but the Jacobin revolution and what lay beyond. For increasingly, except in Tsarist Russia and Turkey, 1789 was no longer a burning issue. At the end of the nineteenth century, Europe consisted overwhelmingly, with the exception of the two absolute monarchies just mentioned and the two republics of France and Switzerland—we need not count some mini-relics of the Middle Ages like San Marino and Andorra—of monarchies that had come to terms with the Revolution, or conversely, of middle classes that had come to terms with old regimes. After 1830 there were no further successful bourgeois revolutions. Nevertheless, the old regimes had learned that survival meant adapting to the age of liberalism and the bourgeoisie—at any rate, to the liberalism of 1789–1791, or rather of 1815–1830. In return they learned that most bourgeois Liberals would, if they could, settle for rather less than their complete programme in return for a guarantee against Jacobinism, democracy, or what it might lead to. In fact, the Restoration monarchy of France in 1814 proved to be the anticipation of a general pattern: an old regime that co-opted enough of the French Revolution to satisfy both partners. As the arch-conservative Bismarck put it in 1866, with his usual incomparable lucidity and taste for provocation: "If there's to be a revolution, it is better that we should make it rather than be its victims."[12]

Bourgeois liberalism (except in Russia and Turkey) no longer needed a revolution and certainly no longer wanted one. In fact it was anxious to move away from the analysis it had previously pioneered, for that analysis, once directed against feudalism, now turned its edge against bourgeois society. As the moderate socialist Louis Blanc had already put it in his *History of the French Revolution* in 1847, the bourgeoisie had won a genuine liberty by means of the revolution, yet the freedom of the people was only nominal.[13] So they needed to make their own French Revolution. More lucid or radical observers went further and saw the class struggle between the new bourgeois ruling class and the proletariat that it exploited as the main content of capitalist history—as that of the bourgeoisie against feudalism had been of the old era. This was the view of the French communists, children of the Jacobin ultraleft of the period after Thermidor. This development of the bourgeois–liberal class analysis was as welcome to social revolutionaries such as Marx as it was unwelcome to its founders. Thierry, shaken by the 1848 Revolution, concluded that class analysis was relevant to the old regime but not to the new one, because the nation, having realised itself through the Revolution, was now a unified whole, one and always the same; and what was even more erroneous was to suppose that the *tiers état* had corresponded to the bourgeoisie, and that this bourgeois *tiers état* was superior to the other lower classes and had interests different from theirs.[14] Guizot, who had always left himself a more effective emergency exit from his class analysis than others, moved sharply away from supporting *any* revolution. Revolutions were or ought to be past history.

On the other hand, for the new proletarian-oriented social

revolutionaries, the question of the bourgeois revolution remained, paradoxically, urgent and vital. It was obvious that bourgeois revolution preceded proletarian revolution, because there had been at least one successful bourgeois revolution and, so far, not yet, a successful proletarian one. It could be and was argued that only the development of capitalism in victorious bourgeois society would create the conditions for the emergence of its proletarian challenger economically and politically for, as Marx put it, commenting on the post-1848 Thierry, "the decisive opposition of the bourgeoisie to the people does not set in until the bourgeoisie ceases as *tiers état*, to oppose the *clergé* and the *noblesse.*"[15] It could also be argued, and later was, that only the extension of the bourgeois revolution to its logical conclusion of the democratic republic would create the institutional and organisational conditions for the effective conduct of the proletarian class struggle against the bourgeoisie. Whatever the details of the argument, it was universally accepted until 1917, at least among the Marxists, that the way to the triumph of the working class and to socialism lay through bourgeois revolution—the necessary first phase of socialist revolution.

Three questions, however, arose at this point. First, it seemed evident that the two must be intertwined. The spectre of communism began to haunt Europe at a time when the bourgeois revolution had either not yet been made (as in Germany), or still seemed far from complete, at least to important sections of the bourgeoisie, let alone the petty bourgeoisie, as in the July monarchy, or even in the Britain of the first Reform Act. Just what was to happen then? This, if you like, was the question for the Left in the 1840s and, while they still hoped for a new 1848, in the 1850s. Second, what was to happen if, as it turned out in many countries, the bourgeoisie gained its main objectives without pushing bourgeois revolution beyond the point of a satisfactory compromise with the old regime? Or, the third contingency, what would occur if it once again sacrificed its political claims to constitution and representative government to some kind of dictatorship to keep the workers at bay? The French Revolution provided material for answers in the first and third of these cases, but not in the second.

Jacobinism seemed the key to the 1848 problem. It seemed *both* essential to the success and survival of the bourgeois revolution, *and* a means of radicalising it and pushing it to the left—beyond its bourgeois limits. In short, it provided both a means of achieving the ends of bourgeois revolution when the unaided bourgeoisie was not in a position to do so, and a means of going beyond it. Marx's initial analysis in the early 1840s—and he was only one of many leftists who scrutinised every phase of the history of the Revolution with a political magnifying glass, in order to discern lessons for the future in it—concentrated on Jacobinism as a political phenomenon that enabled the revolution to jump rather than walk and to achieve in five years what might otherwise have taken it several decades "in view of the timorous and excessively conciliatory conceptions of the bourgeoisie."[16] Yet, in and after 1848, the possibility of pushing the revolution to the left, by means of a political vanguard, of transforming its character, moved into the centre of his thinking: it is this phase of Marx's strategic thought that was to form the starting point of Lenin, or more precisely the Russian revolutionary Marxists who were to find themselves in what seemed to them an analogous situation of a bourgeoisie and a proletariat, both of whom were evidently too weak for the historical tasks assigned to them by their theory. Lenin, his opponents liked to say, was a Jacobin.

Of course the descent of communism from Jacobinism had been the essence of the argument in Buonarroti's *Conspiracy of the Equals* (1828). The French ultraleft took it for granted, before the Blanquists, after 1848, committed themselves to the view that the Hébertists and not the insufficiently atheist Robespierre had been the true revolutionaries, and it was clearly accepted by the young Engels.[17] Both he and Marx initially followed the view that the supporters of the Jacobin

Republic were "the insurgent proletariat," but a proletariat whose victory in 1793–1794 could not but be temporary, and be "an element in the bourgeois revolution itself" so long as the material conditions for the supersession of bourgeois society were not yet mature. (This is, incidentally, one of the rare examples of Marx's use of the actual term *bourgeois revolution*.)[18] The fuller analysis of the social composition of the Paris crowd in 1789–1794 lay far in the future; as did the sharp distinction between Jacobins and sansculottes that was to be so important in the French historiography of the left from Mathiez to Soboul.

In short, it was natural for Marx to tell the Poles in 1848 flatly: "The Jacobin of 1793 has become the Communist of today."[19] And it is thus not surprising that Lenin did not conceal his strong admiration for Jacobinism, and was unconvinced by the Mensheviks who attacked him as a Jacobin in the early 1900s, as well as the Narodniks, who also did so, on other grounds.[20] It should perhaps be added that, unlike so many other Russian revolutionaries, Lenin does not seem to have been steeped in detailed knowledge of the minutiae of French revolutionary history, although, during his wartime exile in Switzerland, he made a reading list on the subject. Practically all he wrote on the topic could be derived from general education and the works of Marx and Engels.

However, quite apart from historical filiation, the Marxian reflection on the strategy of the proletariat in a future post-1848 revolution (as in the Address to the Communist League, 1850)—the famous call for "the revolution in permanence"—provides a link with the kind of political problem the Bolsheviks saw themselves as facing half a century later. Furthermore, Trotsky's critique of Lenin, eventually embodied in the rival orthodoxies of Trotskyist sects, refers back to the same point in Marx's thinking, namely his (occasional) use of the phrase "permanent revolution," for precisely this possibility of transforming bourgeois revolution into something more radical. Marx's original use of this phrase, it need hardly be said, refers directly to the history of the French Revolution.*

It is therefore evident that the question of bourgeois revolution was of substantial practical interest to social revolutionaries, and it became urgent on the rare occasions when they actually found themselves at the head of a revolution. It has remained crucial to them to this day, as witness the debates within the Latin American revolutionary Left since the late 1950s, which have in turn fed into scholarly debate among Latin Americanists, "world-systems" theorists, and "dependency" theorists. We may remind ourselves that the major theoretical issue between the orthodox Soviet-line Communist parties and the various new lefts—dissident Marxist lefts (Trotskyite, Maoist, and Castroite)—was whether the immediate issue was to unite with the national bourgeoisie against regimes dominated by landowners, who could be seen as similar to feudalists, and, of course, against imperialism, or immediately to overthrow the bourgeoisie as well, in order directly to establish a socialist regime.† Although these Third World debates, like analogous debates that split the Indian communist movement, did not refer back to the French Revolution directly, it is clear that they prolonged the debates among Marxists that derive from and can be traced back to that revolution.

The contrast with the Old World is striking. As late as 1946, the Trotskyite version of the debate ("permanent revolution") had been presented in specifically French Revolution terms in Daniel Guérin's *Bourgeois et Bras-Nus*, a work described as a

---

*The most interesting later discussion of Jacobinism from the point of view of a more radical revolution was to be in the prison reflections of Antonio Gramsci. They are reprinted here in an appendix.

†In academic terms this led to endless debates on the nature of the regional mode or modes of production, and arguments about whether Latin America could or could not be regarded as essentially "capitalist" since the conquest, since it formed part of what was claimed as an essentially capitalist world system already in existence in the sixteenth century.

history of class struggles under the First Republic and debated as an exemplification of the permanent revolution thesis.[21]

Yet, suppose the bourgeoisie renounced their intended revolution; or suppose they made it, but felt unable to protect themselves against dangers from the Left under Liberal institutions. What then? The French Revolution provided little guidance in the first case, although, after 1848, it became familiar enough, particularly in central Europe. Historians still argue about whether the German bourgeoisie did indeed abdicate before the Prussian monarchy and nobility, thus (unlike the French or British middle classes) entering upon a *Sonderweg* or a peculiar historical highway that led toward Hitler; or whether in fact they forced Bismarck and the Junkers to grant them a sufficiently bourgeois regime? Whatever the answer to these questions, German Liberals after 1848 settled for considerably less than most of them had regarded as indispensable when they joined the 1848 Revolution. Frederick Engels, in later life, sometimes played with the idea that, on the analogy of France, sooner or later a section of them would really make another bid for uncompromised power, but in fact the new German labour and socialist movement no longer counted on that. However profoundly committed that new movement was to the tradition of the French Revolution—and we should not forget that, before the *Internationale* became its anthem, German workers sang versions of the *Marseillaise*—politically the history of 1789–1794 had ceased to be relevant to the new social-democratic labour parties.[22] It became even less relevant in the industrial countries when their leaders recognised, some more reluctantly than others, that the way forward was not going to lie via the storming of Bastilles, the proclamation of insurrectionary communes, or the like. They were, of course, revolutionary, at least if they were Marxist, as most such parties were. But, as Karl Kautsky, the theoretical guru of the great German SPD, put it, not without a touch of embarrassment: "We are a revolutionary party, but we don't make a revolution."[23]

On the other hand, the French Revolution provided a spectacular example of a retreat into authoritarianism from an excessively radicalised revolution, namely the rise to political power of Napoleon. What is more, the history of France provided a repeat performance of the phenomenon in 1848–1851, when, once again, the moderate Liberals, having defeated an insurrectionary challenge from the Left, were unable to establish conditions of political stability, and created the conditions that allowed another Bonaparte to take power. It is therefore not surprising that the term *Bonapartism* became part of the political vocabulary of social revolutionaries, especially those inspired by Marx, who, in one of his most brilliant pamphlets, described the rise to power by the second Napoleon under the name of the coup d'etat of the first Napoleon. The phenomenon did not escape Liberal observers. Heinrich von Sybel was probably thinking of it when, at the outset of the *History of the French Revolution*, which he began to write in 1853, he thought that the fall of the medieval feudal system (Feudalwesens) everywhere favoured the rise of the modern military state.[24] In 1914 the British Liberal historian and future government minister, H.A.L. Fisher, generalised, not very illuminatingly, about the phenomenon in six lectures under the title *Bonapartism*. More usually, however, the word was used in conventional political discourse, either, as in France, simply to describe the cause of those attached to the Bonaparte dynasty or, more generally, as a synonym for something that could also be called *Caesarism* after Julius Caesar.

However, on the Marxist Left Bonapartism was to be intensively discussed, chiefly in relation to the question of class struggle and class rule in situations of comparative balance between contending class forces. How far, in such situations, could a state apparatus, or even a personal ruler, become autonomous, rising above the classes or playing them off against each other? Although these debates were derived from the experience of the first French Revolution, they really took place at one remove from it, since they were based far more on the experience of the second Bonaparte than on the first. And they were, of course, concerned with political and historical problems increasingly remote from the original Eighteenth Brumaire or even problems of increasing historical generality. Some modern discussions derive little more than the name from the original Bonaparte, as when the term is used to throw light on twentieth-century authoritarian and fascist regimes.[25] Nevertheless, the term returned to political debates concerned much more directly with the Great French Revolution in 1917 and after, as we shall shortly see.

As the nineteenth century proceeded, the experience of the original revolution became increasingly remote from the actual circumstances in which revolutionaries found themselves. This was so even in France. The year 1830 could still be seen—indeed it was—as a successful replay of 1789–1791 by the Liberal bourgeoisie, this time ready for the potential Jacobin danger and therefore able to send the mobilised masses home after a few days before they realised that they had been outwitted. The year 1848 was, once again, easily seen as another variant of the original revolution: this time with a much stronger Jacobin–sansculotte challenge from an ultraleft claiming to represent the new proletariat, but that never had the chance to achieve power even briefly, because it was outvoted, outmanoeuvred, provoked into an isolated insurrection in June 1848, and brutally suppressed. But, as after Thermidor in 1794, the victorious moderates, even when allied with the conservatives, lacked the political support for a stable regime, and gave way to the second Bonaparte. Even the Paris Commune of 1871 still fitted the pattern of the radical revolution of 1792, at least so far as the municipal aspects were concerned: the revolutionary Commune, the popular sections, and so on. If the bourgeoisie no longer thought in terms of 1789–1794, the democratic and social-revolutionary radicals certainly still did. They were, like Blanqui and his followers, steeped in the experience of the 1790s, not to mention neo-Jacobins such as Delescluze who saw themselves as the direct heirs to Robespierre, Saint-Just, and the Committee of Public Safety. There were indeed men in the 1860s whose idea of what to do when Napoleon III fell was to repeat, as exactly as possible, what had happened in the Great Revolution.[26] Whether these parallels with the original revolution made sense or not, they did not seem irrelevant for one major reason: France patently had not succeeded in acquiring a permanent new regime since the fall of the old one in 1789. It had known ten years of the Revolution, fifteen years of Napoleon, another fifteen years of the Restoration, eighteen years of the July monarchy, four years of the Second Republic, and nineteen years of another empire. The Revolution, it seemed, was still going on.

However, it became increasingly clear after 1870 that the formula for a permanent bourgeois regime had been found in the democratic parliamentary republic, although that republic continued to be challenged from time to time. But these were essentially challenges from the Right or, in the case of Boulangism, from something that looked similar to Bonapartism, and therefore actually made it easier to unite the heirs of Liberals and of Jacobins in defence of the Republic and thus to reinforce the policy that, as the late Sanford Elwitt has shown, was systematically pioneered by the moderate opposition in the 1860s.[27] But let us look at the other side of the coin. The fact that bourgeois Liberals could henceforth operate in the framework of a democratic republic, which they had hitherto tried to avoid, demonstrated that the danger of Jacobinism was not, or no longer, what had been feared. The ultras could be integrated into the system—and those who refused could be isolated in a minority ghetto. What Danton or Robespierre had done was no longer of direct operational interest for those inspired by 1792–1794, although, of course, as we have seen, the very co-option of the popular and radical revolution by the moderate Liberals gave its slogans, symbols, and rhetoric enormous national resonance. After all, the date of the most dramatic episode of popular intervention in the Revolution, the taking of the Bastille, was chosen in 1880 as the National Day of the French Republic.

If all this was so in the homeland of the Revolution itself, it was even more obvious elsewhere. Either revolutions were not actually on the political agenda, or they were becoming rather different kinds of revolution. For, even where the politics of insurrection, rebellion, and power emerging from the barrel of the gun were practised or practicable, as on the Iberian peninsula, they were not easily translatable into parallels with 1789–1799. To see this, one has only to look at the career of Giuseppe Garibaldi, who probably took part in as many revolts, revolutions, armed uprisings, and wars of liberation as any man in the nineteenth century, and who, incidentally, began his political career under the influence of the French Revolution, as seen through the prism of the Saint-Simonian ideology, remaining profoundly marked by it.[28] Of course everyone except blinkered reactionaries believed in The Rights of Man and the country that had given them their most influential expression. The military *caudillo* Melgarejo in far-off Bolivia, stronger in political sympathy than in geography and information, offered to rush his cavalry to the aid of France, the country of liberty, when he heard of the Franco-Prussian War of 1870–1871. Nevertheless, admiration or even inspiration is one thing, political models are quite another.

Yet, the French Revolution made a dramatic return as a model, or a point of reference, in Russia, for reasons already suggested. On the one hand, the parallels seemed obvious: an *ancien régime* absolute monarchy in crisis, the need for bourgeois–liberal institutions that, under the circumstances of Tsarism, could *only* be expected through revolution, and more radical revolutionary forces waiting beyond those who only wanted a liberal constitutionalism. On the other hand, revolutionary groups and bodies—one should recall that, under Tsarist conditions, even moderate reformers had to be revolutionaries, since there was no legal way of changing the regime except from the throne—revolutionary groups were steeped in the history of the original French Revolution, and with the strongest incentive to scrutinise its historical record. Here was a revolution that was universally believed to be both inevitable and imminent. Marx himself began to put his money on a Russian upheaval from about 1870 on.

Russian intellectuals, most of whom were necessarily also revolutionaries under the Tsar, were steeped in the history of the French Revolution. "They know the French Revolution better than we do" exclaimed Marcel Cachin, later a grand old man of French communism, to the delegates at the Tours Congress of the Socialist party on his return from Moscow in 1920.[29] Small wonder: the original Russian contributions to the history of the Revolution were substantial. In fact, I.V. Luchitskii (1845–1918), a Russian Liberal, and N.I. Kareiev (1850–1931), a Liberal but originally a Narodnik, were the pioneers in the study of the peasantry and the land question in late-eighteenth-century France, and acknowledged as such by the French. Also the anarchist Peter Kropotkin wrote a two-volume history of the French Revolution that was for long the best serious leftwing history available internationally. It was first published in English and French in 1909, and, finally, in 1914, in Russian.

It is thus no surprise to find that Russian revolutionaries automatically looked for Russian parallels to the French events of 1789–1799, as Plekhanov, the "Father of Russian Marxism," did to the end of his life.[30]

The parallel with the French Revolution, although obvious in the minds of educated participants, does not seem to have been very prominent in the Russian Revolution of 1905, perhaps chiefly because Tsarism, though temporarily shaken, never actually lost control before the revolution was repressed.[31] In 1905 Lenin criticised the Mensheviks as "Girondins" for not even considering the possibility of a Jacobin dictatorship in Russia, but the matter was academic.[32] In any case, Lenin was answering a direct allusion to the experience of the

1793 Convention. After defeat, the relation between working-class and bourgeois revolution was much discussed, with the usual references to Jacobinism and its nature. Nevertheless, the comparison with 1789–1799 did not go much beyond generalities.

On the other hand, 1917 and the years that followed were full of references back to revolutionary France. These went as far as seeking Russian counterparts for the famous figures of the French Revolution. In 1919 W.H. Chamberlin, who was later to write one of the best histories of the Russian Revolution, thought Lenin was like Robespierre, only a "more enlightened mind (with) a more international background," but Charles Willis Thompson, two years later, thought the Lenin–Robespierre parallel was not apt. For Chamberlin, Trotsky was like Saint-Just, but for Thompson he resembled Carnot, the organiser of the revolutionary armies. Further, Thompson dismissed those who saw in Trotsky a Marat.[33]

It would be easy to trace the ways in which historically minded Russian revolutionaries compared the events of their own revolution with its predecessor. Sukhanov, the famous diarist of 1917, is an excellent example of an individual "weaned on the histories of the French and English revolutions," who speculated, as he observed, that the "dual power" of Soviets and Provisional Government would produce some kind of Napoleon or Cromwell—but who, among the revolutionary politicians would be cast for the part?—or perhaps a Robespierre. But, once again, no obvious candidate seemed in sight.[34] Trotsky's own *History of the Russian Revolution* is full of such comparisons, which had undoubtedly been in his mind at the time. The Constitutional Democrats (the chief Liberal party) trying to maintain a constitutional monarchy suggested to him how different 1917 was from 1789; then royal power was still universally accepted, now Tsarism had already lost popular legitimacy. Dual power suggested parallels with the English and French revolutions. In July 1917 the Bolsheviks were manoeuvred into putting themselves at the head of popular demonstrations that they thought mis-timed, and their suppression led to a temporary defeat of the party, and Lenin's flight from Petrograd. The parallel to the demonstrations on the Champ de Mars in July 1791, into which Lafayette had manoeuvred the Republicans, immediately came to Trotsky's mind; as did the parallel between the second and more radical revolution of August 10 1792 and the October revolution, both virtually unresisted, both indeed announced in advance.[35]

It is perhaps more interesting to see how French revolutionary parallels were used by various people to assess, and increasingly to criticise, developments in Russia. Let us remind ourselves, once again, of the historical prototype derived from the French Revolution. It consisted of six phases: the outbreak of the Revolution, that is, the loss of control by the monarchy of the course of affairs in the spring and summer of 1789; the period of the Constituent Assembly ending in the liberal constitution of 1791; the breakdown of the new formula in 1791–1792, due to internal and external tensions, leading to the second revolution of August 10 1792 and the institution of the Republic; third, the radicalisation of the Republic in 1792–1793 while the revolutionary right and left—Gironde and Mountain—fought it out in the new National Convention and the regime struggled against internal revolt and foreign intervention. This culminated in the coup giving power to the Left in June 1793, which introduced the fourth phase: the Jacobin Republic, the most radical phase of the Revolution, and, incidentally (as its popular name implies) the one associated with terror, a succession of internal purges, and an extraordinary and successful total war mobilisation of the people. When France had been saved by this, the radical regime was ended on the 9th of Thermidor. For our purposes, the period from July 1794 until Napoleon's coup can be seen as a single phase, the fifth, which attempted to retreat to a more viable and moderate revolutionary regime. This failed, and on the Eighteenth Brumaire—in 1799—the authoritarian army-based regime of Bonaparte took over. One could no doubt distinguish further between the Napoleonic regime before 1804, when he still ruled as head of a republic, and the later empire, but for the present purposes one need not bother. In any case, for the Restoration Liberals, the entire Napoleonic period belonged to the Revolution. Mignet ended his history of it in 1814.

That the Bolsheviks were the 1917 equivalent of the Jacobins seemed obvious enough. The problem for adversaries of Lenin on the left was that, once the revolution had broken out, the Jacobins were hard to criticise. They were the most consistent and effective revolutionaries, the saviours of France, and, moreover, not to be identified with extremism as such, for Robespierre and the Committee of Public Safety had opposed both enemies to the right and left of them. Hence, old Plekhanov, who did not approve of the October transfer of power, refused to see it as a victory of the Jacobins. He argued that the equivalent of the Hébertists (the ultras who had been liquidated by Robespierre in the spring of 1794), had seized power, and no good could possibly come of it.[36] Conversely, some years later the aged German social-democratic theorist Karl Kautsky also refused the positive link of the Jacobins to the Bolsheviks. Naturally, he argued, friends of Bolshevism pointed to the parallels between the Constitutional Monarchists and the moderate Republican Girondins in the French Revolution, and the defeated Social-Revolutionaries and Mensheviks in Russia, and, therefore, identified the Bolsheviks with the Jacobins. That was to give them credit as true revolutionaries. Although, at the start, the Bolsheviks might have just *looked* like the equivalent of the Jacobins, they had behaved quite differently: they had revealed themselves as Bonapartists, that is, as counterrevolutionaries of sorts.[37]

The stamp of Jacobin authenticity, on the other hand, was given to the Bolsheviks by the most authoritative source: the *Société des Etudes Robespierristes*, which sent the young Revolution the warmest greetings, in the hope that "it would find, to lead it, Robespierres and Saint-Justs capable of safeguarding it against the double danger of weakness and exaggeration."[38] (And, we may add, to continue the war against Germany, which they promptly concluded.) Indeed, the greatest authority on the subject, Albert Mathiez, who saw Lenin as "the Robespierre who succeeded," wrote a pamphlet, *Bolshevism and Jacobinism*, in which he argued that, although history never repeated itself, "the Russian revolutionaries deliberately and consciously copied their French prototypes. They are animated by the same spirit."[39] Mathiez briefly (1920–1922) took his enthusiasm for the Robespierres who succeeded, thanks to a more effective doctrine than the original one, into the new Communist party, a fact which may have cost him the official succession to the Sorbonne Chair when Aulard retired in 1924. Yet it is difficult to see him as a characteristic Marxist or Communist, although the experience of the war effort of 1914–1918 (which he supported) and the Russian Revolution helped to give his synthesis of the history of 1789–1794 (1921) a greater social dimension and political awareness than earlier works of the kind.

Curiously enough, there were few champions of the French revolutionary ultraleft initially. Perhaps they were disarmed by the Bolsheviks' obvious enthusiasm for Marat, after whom the new regime named one of its warships and a street in Leningrad. In any case, a victorious revolution found identification with Robespierre easier than with his guillotined opponents on the left, even though Lenin, shortly after October, defended himself against the accusation of practising a Jacobin terror: "Ours is not the French revolutionary terror which guillotined unarmed people, and I hope we shall not go so far."[40] Alas, the hope proved vain. Not until the triumph of Stalinism did the ultraleft find champions against the new Robespierre of Moscow: among them, Daniel Guérin, whose *La lutte des classes sous la première République* (1946), a curious combination of libertarian and Trotskyist ideas—not without a dash of Rosa Luxemburg—revived the argument that the sansculottes were proletarians struggling against the bourgeois Jacobins.

Indeed, whether or not Stalin saw himself as a Robespierre, foreign Communists in the period of antifascism found it comforting, when considering the Soviet trials and purges, to think they were as justified by necessity as The Terror of 1793–1794 had been.[41] Not least in France, where the idealisation of Robespierre had come to dominate the Jacobin historical tradition, for reasons that have little to do with Marx or Lenin. It was easy enough for French Communists, such as Mathiez, to see Robespierre as "a prefiguration of Stalin."[42] Perhaps in other countries, where the word *Terror* did not so readily suggest episodes of national glory and revolutionary triumph, this parallel with Stalin would have been avoided. Still, it is hard not to agree with Isaac Deutscher that Stalin "belonged to the family of great revolutionary despots, with Cromwell, Robespierre and Napoleon."[43]

However, the debate on Jacobinism itself was not very significant. There was actually little doubt that, if anyone in 1917 represented the equivalent of the Jacobins, it was the Bolsheviks. The real problem was: where was the Bonaparte or Cromwell, who historical precedent suggested might be somewhere in the wings? Furthermore, would there be a Thermidor, and if so, where would it lead Russia?

The first of these was seen as a very real possibility in 1917 itself. Kerensky has been so totally extruded from history that I remember my own sense of amazement at being told that the little elderly gentleman who could be seen walking around the Hoover Library in Stanford, was he. One somehow felt he should have been dead for generations, although, in actual fact, he was at that time not yet eighty. His moment in history lasted from March to November of 1917, but during this period he was a central figure, as is shown by the persistent debates, at that time and later, about his desire or ability to be a Bonaparte. These clearly became part of the Soviet heritage for, years later, both Trotsky and M.N. Roy argued, in the context of the general question of Bonapartism and the Russian Revolution, that Kerensky's attempt to play Napoleon proved to be an abortion, because no base for it had yet been laid by the prior development of the Revolution.[44] These arguments were based on the attempt—briefly successful—by the Provisional Government to suppress the Bolsheviks in the summer of 1917. What was in Kerensky's mind at the time was almost certainly not turning himself into a Napoleon, but rather resurrecting another aspect of the French Revolution, namely, launching a Jacobin-type call for a war of patriotic resistance against Germany that would keep Russia in the Great War. The trouble was that all the real revolutionaries, and not only the Bolsheviks, opposed the war because they knew that the demand for Bread, Peace, and Land was what actually moved most of the masses. Kerensky did issue his call, and once again launched the Russian army into an offensive in the summer of 1917. It misfired totally and cut the Provisional Government's throat. The peasant soldiers refused to fight, went home, and started to divide up the land. The people who actually succeeded in getting the Russians to fight again were the Bolsheviks: but *after* the October Revolution and *after* pulling out of the World War. Here the parallel between Jacobins and Bolsheviks was obvious. W.H. Chamberlin rightly noted, in the middle of the Russian Civil War, the similarities between the Jacobin success in building up formidable revolutionary armies out of conscripts on the ruins of the old royal army, and "the equally striking contrast between the helpless, disorderly mob that threw down its arms and refused to fight before Brest-Litowsk and the resolute, effective Red Army that drove the Czechoslovaks from the Volga and the French from the Ukraine."[45]

However, the real debate about Bonapartism and Thermidor set in *after* the October Revolution, and among the various sectors of Soviet and non-Soviet Marxism. Paradoxically, one might say that these debates prolonged the effective historical memory and influence of the French Revolution, which would otherwise have been transferred into the museum of past history in most parts of the world, except, of course, in France. For, after all, 1917 became the prototype of the great twentieth-century revolution, the one with which the politics of this century has had to come to terms. The sheer scale and international repercussions of the Russian Revolution dwarfed those of 1789, and there was no precedent for its major innovation, namely a social revolutionary regime that deliberately went beyond the bourgeois democratic phase, *and that maintained itself permanently and proved capable of generating others.* The Jacobinism of the Year II, whatever its social character, was a temporary episode. The 1871 Commune of Paris, although clearly a working-class phenomenon, was not much of a regime at all and barely lasted a few weeks. Its potential for socialist or other postbourgeois transformation rests entirely on Karl Marx's eloquent obituary of it, which became so important a text for both Lenin and Mao. Until 1917, even Lenin, like most Marxists, did not expect or envisage an immediate, direct transition to "proletarian power" as a consequence of the overthrow of Tsarism. Yet, since 1917 and for most of the twentieth century, it is precisely postcapitalist regimes that have been expected to be the normal consequence of revolutions. Indeed, in the Third World 1917 largely blanketed out 1789: what kept it alive as a political point of reference, and thus gave it a new lease on life at second hand, was its role in the internal debates of Soviet Russia itself.

Thermidor was the obvious term used to describe any development that marked a political retreat of revolutionaries from radical to moderate positions, which revolutionaries usually (but wrongly) identified with a betrayal of the revolution. The Mensheviks, who had refused from the start to go along with Lenin's project for transforming the bourgeois revolution into a proletarian one, on the far from unreasonable grounds that Russia was not ready for the construction of socialism, were ready to detect Thermidor from the start—in the case of Martov, as early as 1918. Everyone naturally recognised it when the Soviet regime initiated NEP (New Economic Policy) in 1921, and hailed that "Thermidor" with varying degrees of self-satisfaction if they were critics of the regime and varying degrees of foreboding if they were Bolsheviks (who equated Thermidor with counterrevolution).[46] The term was readily used against proponents of NEP as a possible way forward rather than a temporary retreat, such as Bukharin. From 1925 on it came to be used by Trotsky and his allies against the party majority, as a general accusation that the revolution was being betrayed, embittering the already tense relations between the groups. Although the arrow of "Thermidorian reaction" was originally aimed at the Bukharin perspective of socialist development, and therefore missed its target once Stalin entered on the opposite course of ultrarapid industrialisation and collectivisation in 1928, Trotsky returned to the cry of "Thermidor" in the 1930s, when, admittedly, his political judgment had gone to pieces. One way or another Thermidor remained the weapon with which Trotsky attacked his opponents—suicidally so, for, at crucial moments it made him regard the politically hapless Bukharin as a greater danger than Stalin. Indeed, while Trotsky never quite gave up the slogan, in retrospect he came close to admitting that he and his allies had been blinded by the analogy of 1794.[47]

The Thermidorian analogy, to quote Isaac Deutscher, generated "indescribable heat and passion in all factions" in the struggle between Lenin's death and Stalin's triumph.[48] Deutscher, who has described this atmosphere unusually well in his biography of Trotsky, also suggests plausible explanations for the "uncannily violent passions which this bookish historical reminiscence aroused."[49] For, like the French Revolution between Thermidor and Brumaire, Soviet Russia between 1921 and 1928 was visibly living in an interim. Even though Bukharin's policy of transformation on the basis of NEP, justified by appeals to the late Lenin, is today seen as the

57

historical legitimation of the Gorbachev reform policies, in the 1920s it was merely one of the policy options for the Bolsheviks, and, as it turned out, a losing one. Nobody knew what would happen, or what ought to happen, if the makers of the revolution were in a position to control it. In Deutscher's words "It brought to their minds the uncontrollable element in revolution, of which they were increasingly, if dimly, aware" and to which I shall shortly refer.[50]

Although, in retrospect, the 1920s seem to Soviet observers of the 1980s a brief era of economic hope and cultural liveliness before Russia's iron age of Stalin, to Old Bolsheviks at the time it was a nightmare of sorts, in which familiar things became strange and menacing: the hope of a socialist economy turned out to be just the old Russia of *muzhiks*, small traders, and bureaucrats, only minus the aristocracy and the old bourgeoisie; the Party, that band of brothers devoted to the world revolution, turned out to be the one-party system of power, obscure and impenetrable even to those who formed part of it. "The Bolshevik of 1917 would hardly recognize himself in the Bolshevik of 1928," wrote Christian Rakovsky.[51]

The struggles for the future of the Soviet Union, and perhaps for world socialism, were fought out by small groups and factions of politicians amid the massive indifference of an ignorant peasantry and the terrible apathy of the working class in whose name the Bolsheviks claimed to act. Here, for the connoisseurs of the French Revolution, was the most obvious parallel with Thermidor. According to Rakovsky, the Third Estate had disintegrated once it had defeated the old regime.[52] The social base of the revolution had narrowed, even under the Jacobins, and power was exercised by ever fewer people. The hunger and misery of the people in the time of crisis did not allow the Jacobins to trust the fate of the revolution to the popular vote. Robespierre's arbitrary and terroristic rule drove the people into political indifference, and it was this that had enabled the Thermidorians to overthrow his regime. Whatever the outcome of the struggles fought by tiny handfuls of

Bolsheviks over the inert body of the Soviet masses—as Rakovsky wrote after Stalin's victory—it would not be influenced from below. Indeed, Rakovsky bitterly quoted the Babeuf of the Thermidor period: "To re-educate the people in the love of liberty is more difficult than to win liberty."[53]

Logically, in such a situation, the student of the French Revolution should have expected a Bonaparte. Indeed Trotsky eventually saw Stalin and Stalinism in this light, although initially, once again, his closeness to the French precedent clouded his judgment and led him to think a *literal* Eighteenth Brumaire probable, namely an army coup against Stalin.[54] Yet, paradoxically, the accusation of Bonapartism was chiefly used by opponents of Trotsky as a natural counter to the accusations of Thermidor. Trotsky had, after all, been the chief architect and effective head of the Red Army, and was himself, as usual, sufficiently aware of the precedent to resign as War Commissar in 1925 to counter charges that he harboured Bonapartist ambitions.[55] Stalin's own initiative in these accusations was probably negligible, although no doubt he welcomed and used them. There is no evidence in his works or record that he had any special interest in the French Revolution. His historical references are, essentially, to Russian history.

Thus, the struggle of the 1920s in the Soviet Union was conducted with mutual accusations taken from the French Revolution. It is, incidentally, a warning against an excessive tendency to look for history to repeat itself. Insofar as it was a mere exchange of insults, the mutual accusations of Thermidor and Bonapartism were politically irrelevant. Insofar as those who made them actually took their analogies with 1789–1799 seriously, they were far more often than not misled by them. Yet they indicate the extraordinary depth of the Russian revolutionaries' immersion in the history of their predecessors. It is not so significant that a Trotsky should cite what an insignificant Jacobin (Brival) said in the National Convention on the day after Thermidor, in his defence before the Control

Commission in 1927—an occasion that contained a more prophetic reminiscence of the Revolution, namely a warning of the guillotine to come in the 1930s.[56] What is more striking is that the first man publicly to make the parallel between post-Lenin Russia and Thermidor was not an intellectual, but the secretary of the Leningrad party organisation in 1925, a self-taught worker, Peter Zalutsky.[57]

Yet there was one important distinction between Thermidor and Bonapartism as slogans. Everybody was against military dictators. If there was one fundamental principle among Marxist revolutionaries—and no doubt the memory of Napoleon contributed to it—it was the need for the absolute supremacy of the civilian party over the military, however revolutionary. That, after all, was the reason for the institution of the Political Commissars. At most one might argue that Bonaparte had not actually betrayed the revolution but made it irreversible by institutionalising it in his regime. There were heterodox Communists—M.N. Roy was one—who asked: "So what if the proletarian revolution of our day is going to have its Napoleonism? It may be a necessary stage."[58] Yet such sentiments were apologetic.

On the other hand, Thermidor can be seen not as a mere betrayal of the Revolution or a way of bringing it to an end, but as a shift from short-term crisis to longer-term transformation: both a retreat from an untenable position and an advance into a more viable strategy. After all, the people who overthrew Robespierre in the original Ninth Thermidor were not counterrevolutionaries, but his own comrades and colleagues in the National Convention and the Committee of Public Safety. In the history of the Russian Revolution there is an obvious moment when the Bolsheviks were forced to do something very similar, although without sacrificing any of their leaders.

The ruthless "War Communism" by which the Soviet government had raised the resources to survive the Civil War of 1918–1920 corresponded to the analogous emergency policies of the Jacobin war effort, even to the extent that there were, in both cases, revolutionary enthusiasts who saw the enforced austerities of the period as a first instalment of their utopia, whether defined as the rule of a spartan and egalitarian Virtue or in some more Marxist manner. In both cases, victory made the crisis regimes politically intolerable and, indeed, unnecessary. Under the pressure of revolt by both workers and peasants the New Economic Policy had to be instituted in 1921. It was certainly a retreat for the Revolution, although an unavoidable one. Yet could it not also be seen as, or transformed into, a planned shift to a necessarily less dramatic, but in the long run more firmly based, mode of its development? Lenin's own views were not firm or consistent, but—always the supreme political realist—he increasingly threw his weight behind the policy of postrevolutionary reform and gradualism. What exactly was in his mind, especially in his last two years, when his condition made it increasingly impossible for him to write, and in the end even to speak, is the subject of much debate.[59] Nevertheless, the man who wrote: "What is new at the present moment for our revolution is the need to resort to a 'reformist,' gradualist, cautiously roundabout method of activity in the fundamental questions of economic construction" was not thinking in terms of sudden drama.[60] It is equally certain that Lenin had no intention of abandoning the construction of a socialist society, even though in his last published article he said "we ... lack enough civilisation to enable us to pass straight on to socialism, although we do have the political requisites for it."[61] Until the end of his life he was confident that socialism in the world would eventually triumph.

It is thus not surprising that, in the atmosphere of Gorbachev's Soviet Union, Lenin has been credited with a more positive view of Thermidor than the usual one; even with the idea that one of the main problems of the Revolution was how to ensure its own "auto-Thermidorization."[62] In the absence of any documentation, one must express scepticism. The connotation of the word *Thermidor* in contemporary Bolshevik and international Communist usage was so uniformly and strongly negative, that one would be surprised to find Lenin using such a term, although perhaps not more surprised than to find him asking the Bolsheviks to be reformists. However, even if he did not, the reference to "auto-Thermidorization" in the Moscow of 1988–1989 is evidence of the strength and persistence of the French Revolution as a point of reference for its great successor.

Beyond Thermidor and Bonaparte, Jacobins and The Terror, the French Revolution suggested more general parallels with the Russian Revolution, or indeed with subsequent major social revolutions. One of the first things observed about it was that it resembled not so much a set of planned decisions and controlled actions by human beings, but a natural phenomenon that was not under, or escaped from, human control. In our century we have grown accustomed to other historical phenomena that have this characteristic: both world wars, for instance. What actually happens in such cases, how they develop, what their outcome is, have practically nothing to do with the intentions of those who made the initial decisions. They have their own dynamics, their own unpredictable logic. In the 1790s the counterrevolutionaries were probably the first to draw attention to this uncontrollability of the revolutionary process, since it provided them with arguments against the supporters of the Revolution. However, revolutionaries themselves made the same observation, comparing the Revolution to natural cataclysms. "The lava of revolution flows on majestically, sparing nothing" wrote the German Jacobin Georg Forster in Paris in October 1793. The revolution, he claimed, "has broken all dams, risen above all barriers, erected by many of the best intellects, here and elsewhere . . . whose systems prescribed its limits." The revolution simply was "the Revolution, a natural phenomenon too rare for us to know its peculiar laws."[63] Of course the metaphor of a natural phenomenon cut both ways. If it suggested catastrophe to conservatives, it was an inevitable, an unstoppable catastrophe. It was something that, intelligent conservatives soon realised, could not simply be suppressed but had to be canalised and tamed.

Time and again we find the natural metaphor applied to revolutions. I do not suppose Lenin even knew of the many such passages about the French Revolution when he wrote, shortly after October, about the situation before the fall of Tsarism: "We were aware that the old power was on top of a volcano. Many signs told us of the great work going on deep down in people's minds. We felt the air was charged with electricity. We were sure it would inevitably explode in a purifying thunderstorm."[64] What other metaphor than that of a volcanic eruption, or a hurricane, would come so spontaneously to the mind?

But for the revolutionaries, and especially for one as ruthlessly realistic as Lenin, the consequences of the nature-like uncontrollability of the phenomenon were practical. He was, in fact, the very opposite of the Blanquist or the man who tries to make revolution by an act of will or a coup or putsch, although it is for this that his opponents criticised him. He was at the opposite pole from Fidel Castro and Che Guevara. Time and again, and particularly in and after 1917, he insisted that "revolutions cannot be made, they cannot be taken in turns. A revolution cannot be made to order, it develops."[65] Or "revolution can never be forecast, it cannot be foretold; it comes of itself. Did anyone know even a week before the February revolution that it was about to break out?"[66] Or "no sequence can be established for revolutions."[67] When some Bolsheviks were prepared to gamble on the outbreak of the revolution in western Europe, to which indeed Lenin also pinned his hopes, he repeated, over and over again, that "we do not know and *cannot know* any of this. *No one* is in a position to know," whether there would be a delay, how soon revolution would sweep the West, whether it or the Bolsheviks would be defeated by reaction, or what would take place.[68] The party had to be prepared for all contingencies and adjust its strategies and tactics to circumstances as they arose.

But was there not a risk that, in navigating the stormy seas and currents of history, the revolutionaries would find themselves carried not merely in directions unintended and unpredicted, but *away* from their original objective? It is only in this sense that we can speak of what Furet calls *dérapage*, which can be seen not as a diversion from the course of the vehicle, but rather as the discovery that the lie of the historical land is such that, given the situation and place and conditions under which a revolution occurs, even the best driver cannot take it in the desired direction. For this, after all, was one of the lessons of the French Revolution. Nobody in 1789 intended the Jacobin dictatorship, The Terror, Thermidor, or Napoleon. Nobody from the most moderate reformers to the most radical agitators would in 1789 have actually welcomed any of these developments, except, perhaps, the ominous Marat, who, in spite of David's wonderful painting, was by no means universally mourned among his revolutionary colleagues. Did not Lenin's very commitment to taking *any* decision, however disagreeable, that guaranteed the survival of the revolution, his very refusal to let ideology stand in the way of doing what had to be done, run the risk of turning the revolution into something else?

As we have seen, this fear may have dimly haunted the Bolsheviks after Lenin's death. It is one of the many signs of his own greatness, that Lenin himself was prepared frankly to confront this possibility when, in the memoirs that are so valuable an eyewitness account of the revolution, it was suggested by Sukhanov. It is significant that, in confronting it, Lenin fell back, once again, on the period of the French Revolution. He quoted Napoleon's famous maxim: "First get into battle, and then see what's to be done" ("On s'engage et puis on voit"). We got into battle, the dying Lenin dictated in 1923. Well, we found we had to do things we hated doing and would not willingly have done—making the peace at Brest

Litowsk, retreating to the New Economic Policy "and so forth."[69] We cannot quite blame him for refusing to go into the details of that "and so forth" or for insisting that these diversions and setbacks were "details of development (from the standpoint of world history they were certainly details)."[70] One could hardly have expected him not to express faith in the Revolution and its long-term prospects—even though we know how great he thought the difficulties were, how far more remote the prospects of advance, how narrow the "peasant limitations" confining the regime.

But Lenin's faith in the future of the Russian Revolution also rested on history: the history of the French Revolution. For, as we have seen, the main lesson nineteenth-century observers drew from it, was that it was not an event but a process. To reach what Lenin and most Marxists regarded as the logical, "classical" outcome of a bourgeois revolution, namely a democratic parliamentary republic, took almost a century. 1789 was not the Revolution, and neither was 1791 or 1793–1794, or the Directory, or Napoleon, or the Restoration, or 1830, or 1848, or the Second Empire. All these were phases of the complex and contradictory process of creating the permanent framework of a bourgeois society in France. Why should Lenin in 1923 not have assumed that the Russian Revolution would not also be a lengthy historical process, with its difficult zigzags and setbacks?

How Soviet observers look at this process today, after some seventy years, it is impossible to say. The Babel of discordant voices that now has a chance, for the first time since the Revolution, to emerge from the country, cannot yet be historically analysed into its components. One thing, however, is clear. The French revolutionary analogy is still alive. Given the history of the Soviet Union, we could hardly expect it not to be. The history of the French Revolution itself is being reconsidered. It is fairly certain that Robespierre will be a rather less positive hero in the Soviet historiography than he was in the past. But in the bicentenary of the French Revolution

65

there was another parallel that struck intellectuals in Gorbachev's Russia as the first genuinely elected Congress of People's Deputies of the country opened. It was the calling of the States General and their transformation into a National Assembly that set out to reform the realm of France. That analogy is no more realistic than other attempts to see the pattern of one historic event in another. It also lends itself to different readings and emphases, depending on the current political stance of whoever makes it. We need not agree with the version of one democratic reformer who, in mid-1989 after his side had been outvoted in the Moscow Congress, wrote: "Today, when the French events of two centuries ago are in our minds—and Gorbachev has stated that *perestroika* is a revolution—I would like to recall that the 'Third Estate' also constituted a third of the deputies, but it was that third which became the authentic National Assembly."[71] Nevertheless, there could be no greater tribute to the surviving political significance of the Revolution of 1789 than that it should still provide a model and point of reference for those wishing to transform the Soviet system. In 1989, 1789 remains, or has once again become, more relevant than 1917, even in the country of the Great October Revolution.

From One Centenary to Another

The first chapter of this book considered what the nineteenth-century Liberal bourgeoisie made of the French Revolution. The second followed those who feared, or made, or hoped to make, a revolution that took them beyond the Jacobins and, therefore, assimilated the experience of the years from 1789 on. For, it can never be repeated often enough that, both liberalism and social revolution, both bourgeoisie and, at least potentially, proletariat, both democracy (in whatever version) and dictatorship, found their ancestors in the extraordinary decade that began with the calling of the States General, the storming of the Bastille, and the *Declaration of the Rights of Man and Citizen.*

Everyone except the conservatives could look back on some part of it, or interpret its history in a way suitable to their cause. French politics, as we know, continued to be played as a costume drama in Phrygian bonnets. Moderate Liberals could be recognised because their hero was Mirabeau or the Girondins, about whom a famous but vapid romantic poet and politician, Alphonse Lamartine (1790–1869) published a multivolume history on the eve of the 1848 Revolution, intended to discourage the excesses of Jacobinism. When the

Revolution broke out, Lamartine did his best to sidetrack leftwing radicals and later to suppress them. Mainstream Republicans, following Michelet and Auguste Comte, chose Danton as their hero. Leftwing Republicans and insurrectionaries picked Marat or, increasingly, Robespierre as their man, except for the most impassioned atheists, who could not swallow his championship of a Supreme Being. It has been suggested that the identification of the great figures of the Revolution with later, and bitterly conflicting, political positions made it impossible for France to develop a cult of the Founding Fathers, as was the case in the United States. As far as I am aware, none of them has ever appeared on a postage stamp.[1]

Conversely, these differences were not significant for the Russian Bolsheviks, provided the figures were revolutionary enough. They did not even have to be ancestors of socialism. When the Bolsheviks had come to power in Russia, Lenin thought it important to educate a largely illiterate population in politics and therefore proposed, in 1918, that monuments to various persons who had deserved well of the Revolution should be put up in conspicuous places in cities, especially where soldiers could see them, together with short biographical tablets. They naturally included Socialists and Communists—Marx, Engels, Lassalle—Russian Radicals and precursors—Radishchev, Herzen, Perovskaya—general all-purpose liberators such as Garibaldi, and progressive poets. Among the figures from the French Revolution, which were extremely prominent, we find both Robespierre and Danton, equally nonsocialist, but—as far as I can discover—no Babeuf. For Lenin's purposes victorious revolutionaries, however shortlived, were clearly more important than their ideological positions. It appears that this commemoration of French revolutionaries as ancestors of the October Revolution was a brief episode. Most of these have disappeared since, for reasons of speed, artists were authorised to produce their sculptures in plaster and terracotta, until more permanent bronze or marble works could be created. However, one relief of Robespierre, made in 1920 by the creator of the monuments to Robespierre, Danton, and Herzen in Leningrad, still exists to suggest what has been lost.[2] Incidentally, the French Revolution does not seem to have played an important part in the later iconography or toponymy of Soviet Russia.

In short, everybody had his or her French Revolution, and what was celebrated, condemned, or rejected in it, depended not on the politics and ideology of 1789 but on the commentator's own time and place. This refraction of the Revolution through contemporary political prisms is the subject of this chapter. It is only too evident, as we shall see, in the debates and conflicts that surrounded the revolutionary bicentenary in 1989, or, indeed the first centenary, celebrated in 1889.

Nobody had the slightest doubt that this was, both nationally and internationally, a supremely political occasion. The ambassadors of Russia, Italy, Austria-Hungary, Germany, and Britain—that is, of all the great powers other than France—refused pointedly to attend the celebration of the anniversary of the meeting of the States General (which was chosen to mark the start of the Revolution); although *Le Temps* pointed out bitterly that their predecessors *had* attended the first anniversary of the taking of the Bastille in 1790. *The Times* of London had no doubt they were correct. "Unfortunately," it thought, "the Revolution which had commenced under such brilliant auspices, instead of making reforms, ended in the reign of terror, confiscation and proscription, and the decapitation of the King and Queen." So, although other nations "which gradually adopted the reforms introduced by the Revolution" were not actually refusing to celebrate the centenary, because lesser diplomats had not been recalled, the ambassadors could hardly, as personal representatives of their monarchs, be expected by their presence to express their approval of the Jacobins.[3] Moreover, the French Republic had intended to celebrate the centenary of its founding event not only with a ceremony or two, but with the then habitual international exposition—a particularly striking one, since its chief monument, the newly constructed Eiffel Tower, is still internationally the single most widely known building in France. Yet there was heavy pressure on the French and, as *The Times* once again reported, with approval, "Gradually, under the influence of public good sense at home and abroad [that is, the threat of boycott], the Exhibition has dropped its intimate connexion with the Revolution" so that its inauguration was no longer a part of the official centenary celebration.[4]

Naturally there were countries in which the centenary was a less controversial event, for instance the United States, where New York decorated its statues for the centennial celebration of the fall of the Bastille.[5] A Republic born in revolution and linked with the French Revolution via Lafayette and Tom Paine did not find the mere fact of revolution so hard to swallow. Nevertheless the young, but already statesmanlike, Woodrow Wilson—the later President— then teaching history at Bryn Mawr, saw Jacobinism as a most unsatisfactory example to put before the eyes of anyone, especially Latin Americans. However, outside the western hemisphere, monarchies were still the almost universal form of government and, if only for this reason, those who ruled states were highly sensitive about the celebration of regicide.

Nevertheless, the major controversial issue raised by the centennial was not monarchy but democracy. This is what the argument was about, rather than terror, proscription (that is, the persecution of dissidents), or even the most awful nightmare of nineteenth-century bourgeois society: confiscation of private property. France had finally chosen to be a republic and a democracy in the 1870s. Its rulers had deliberately chosen to define themselves as the heirs of the Revolution, by making 14 July into the National Day and choosing the *Marseillaise* as the national anthem; and, in spite of a certain reluctance to recall Robespierre, after whom, even today, few streets in France are named, the Republic did not exclude the Jacobin inheritance. It actually elected a man who bore one of the great Jacobin names to the presidency in 1887—the grandson of Lazare Carnot, the Trotsky of the revolutionary armies—although, of course, the Jacobin achievement in winning military supremacy for France was the least controversial aspect of that regime. On this left and centre could agree, which is why the prominent figures of the Year II, formally placed in the Pantheon in 1889 on the anniversary of the abolition of feudalism, were three men of war, Carnot, Hoche, and Marceau.[6] Still, if the official centenary carefully avoided recalling the more controversial dates after the proclamation of the Republic on 21 September 1792, and concentrated—as did the second—on the first three months of the Revolution in 1789, it did not disclaim any of it. The only historiographic act of the Republic in 1889 was to vote funds for a national edition of Michelet's Jacobin *History of the French Revolution*. The municipality of Paris, then more radical, went further: it erected a statue to Danton, which still stands by the Odéon metro stop, on the site of the house where Danton himself had been arrested in 1794.

Jacobinism was the touchy part of the Revolution and, in 1889, Jacobinism meant democracy. For, although Socialists and other revolutionaries were certainly for it, and although the Second International was actually founded in Paris in 1889—fully conscious of the significance of the date and the place—socialism was not yet a major political force in the first half of 1889, except in Germany. It was soon to become so, but not until after the centennial. Democracy was what worried observers.

For there is one big difference between the first and second centennials. Except for democracy, nobody from the Liberals leftward saw the Revolution as other than a major historical event, with major achievements that were judged, on the whole, positively. "The principles of the French Revolution" wrote an author in the *Contemporary Review*, "have become the common property of the civilized world." That he wrote, remembering the Glorious Revolution of 1688, "clothed in historical form they were English long before they became French" simply proves that he approved of them.[7] The revolution, thought the historian and Liberal Catholic Lord Acton, who lectured on it at Cambridge in the 1890s, marked "an immense onward step in the march of mankind, a thing to which we are all today indebted for some of the political benefits we enjoy."[8] An intelligent and worried Liberal, Anatole Leroy-Beaulieu, invented a centennial banquet at which various foreigners gave their generally critical opinions about the Revolution, but the surprising thing about them is how much of it they accepted.[9] The American guest naturally claimed that, if anyone had invented liberty, it was his people and not France. The British guest, supposed to be a Liberal Unionist baronet of Whig family, naturally claimed the same. The German congratulated himself that his country had not had a revolution and had defeated the sixteenth-century peasant war that could have been one, but the Revolution had hastened German national development. And if it was so universally hailed by the great minds of Germany, it was because these were already imbued with the principles that they thought they saw the French put into action. The Italian hailed the Revolution's contribution to the risorgimento and the reconstitution of modern nationalities, but of course found both its good and bad elements already present in the Italian tradition. The Greek, obviously, referred back to the classical tradition, while also paying tribute to the Revolution's contribution to reviving his country. And so on. In short, the criticisms of Leroy-Beaulieu's guests—and they clearly are not only mouthpieces for the author's own—assume the general acceptance and acceptability, at least in the West, of the Revolution's principles.

Those who thought the Revolution was a disaster—"the tremendous catastrophe of 1789 followed by a hundred years of revolution" as the *Edinburgh Review* called it—did so because

of the popular element in it that was identified with Jacobinism.[10] But although there were the obligatory references to
The Terror, the real enemy was "the principle that the
popular will is over all persons and all institutions supreme" as
Henry Reeve, an old British friend of Guizot, Thiers, and de
Tocqueville put it, when reviewing Hippolyte Taine's passionately antirevolutionary *Origins of Contemporary France*, which
had appeared recently.[11] For, thought Henry Reeve, if that
principle were accepted "there is an end not only of what are
called constitutional barriers, but of the very bases of civil
society and the fundamental laws of morality."[12] And, indeed,
as another reviewer of Taine's book put it, its central political
lesson was distrust of democratic principles of government.[13]
Although one might suppose that the word *anarchy*, which
came readily to the lips of anti-Jacobin writers, referred to
bloodshed and lawlessness, in fact they had something less
dramatic in mind. The *Edinburgh Review* spoke of a gradual
descent, over the past one hundred years "to a condition of
anarchy which threatens the very existence of the nation" in
France.[14] This obviously was not intended to mean that Paris,
let alone Burgundy, in 1889 approximated to the condition of
the South Bronx in 1989, even though the author thought,
giving no evidence, that the government's anticlericalism
meant "a great relaxation of morals and a singular increase of
crime."[15] What he meant, and what others of his sympathies
meant, was that a century of revolution had given France
"universal suffrage without intelligence," to quote Goldwin
Smith who therefore saw the Revolution as "the greatest
calamity to befall the human race."[16] Universal suffrage, to
return to the *Edinburgh Review*, "has gradually undermined the
authority of the enlightened classes." Unnecessarily so, for—as
Smith wrote—"what the mass of us want is not a vote ... but
strong, stable, enlightened and responsible government."[17]
The Revolution — here the reference is to Burke—had
drastically broken with tradition, and thus removed the
safeguards against anarchy.[18]

The note of hysteria in these attacks may seem to us exaggerated, especially as even severe anti-Jacobins did not deny—in this they differed from the anti-Jacobins of 1989—that the Revolution had done France some good. It had "tremendously increased the material wealth of the nation."[19] It had given France a solid body of peasant proprietors, always regarded in the nineteenth century as an element of political stability.[20] When we actually analyse these antirevolutionary texts, we find that the worst they can say is that France, since the Revolution, had become politically unstable—no regime lasting for more than twenty years, thirteen different constitutions in a century, and so on.[21] To be fair, in the centenary year the Republic was in the midst of a serious crisis, the political movement of General Boulanger, which could not but make observers think of earlier military men who had put an end to unstable republics. Yet, whatever one thought about French politics in the 1880s and 1890s, it seems quite absurd to speak of that country in apocalyptic terms in 1889. It was recognisably the same country that, twenty years later—when Boulanger, Panama, and Dreyfus were still living memories—*The Spectator*, reviewing another book on the French Revolution, could describe as "the soundest, the most stable, as well as the most civilized of Continental countries."[22]

What aroused all these terrors and passions was not the state to which France had been reduced after a century of revolution, but the knowledge that democratic politics, and all they implied, were now spreading in all bourgeois countries, and "universal suffrage without intelligence" was sooner or later bound to come. That is what Goldwin Smith meant when he said that "Jacobinism ... is now as established a disease as the smallpox. The infection is beginning to cross the Channel."[23] This was the period when electoral democracy on a broad base became, for the first time, an integral part of the politics of even those countries that we today think of as the most traditionally democratic; that is, when the sort of liberal constitutionalism that bourgeois Liberals such as Guizot had

instituted precisely as a *barrier* to democracy, where the poor
and the ignorant (not to mention all women) were excluded
from the vote *on principle*, was politically no longer tenable.
What is not so widely known is how enormously worried the
ruling classes were about the implications of electoral democracy. They looked at the United States, as de Tocqueville had
done, but unlike de Tocqueville they saw primarily the best
Congress and the best city governments that money could
buy: graft, spoils, demagogy, and political machines—also, in
the period of the disturbed 1880s, social discontent and
agitation. They looked at France, and they saw, in the long
shadow of Robespierre, corruption, instability, demagogues,
although not political machines. In short, they saw the crisis of
states and politics hitherto known. No wonder the centenary
of the Revolution filled them with foreboding.

Yet, if we leave aside genuine reactionaries such as the
Catholic Church of the 1864 Syllabus and the First Vatican
Council, which rejected everything in the miserable nineteenth century, the French Revolution did not in general
rouse rejections as hysterical as those I have quoted. Taine's
Origins of Contemporary France was generally regarded, at least in
the Anglo-Saxon world, as over the top, even by those who
sympathised with its anti-Jacobinism. Reviewers asked some
sensible questions. Why did Taine not see that in 1789 it could
not have been as obvious to Frenchmen as it was now, that a
change to Liberal institutions was possible without a fundamental revolution?[24] Why did he not see that the key to the
situation was that not even the Moderates could trust the
king? If everyone was so devoted to the monarchy, why did
France, which was not Republican in 1788, never become
royalist again?[25] Taine did not recognise the dilemma of each
party as it came to power: "Reliance on the support of the
Paris mob meant connivance at outrage and crimes which
made it impossible to establish free institutions in France.
Repression of the Parisian mob meant reaction, and, probably
enough, the restoration of despotism."[26] In fact, with all due

respect to him as an intellectual heavyweight, Taine's work was considered propagandist rather than scientific. The bitterness of the conservative, thought *The Spectator*, overflowed into his book. He "lacks scientific disinterestedness, breadth of view and insight," wrote *The Nation*. Eminent French intellectuals have usually been received abroad with greater respect than this one.[27]

Let us now turn from the first centenary to the background of the second. The first thing to note about the intervening century is that we now know incomparably more about the history of the French Revolution than was known in 1889. One of the chief consequences, not so much of the first centenary as of the adoption, by the Third Republic, of the Revolution as its founding event, was that its historiography surged forward. In the 1880s France acquired not only a museum of the Revolution—the Carnavalet Museum in Paris—but in 1885 a lectureship, in 1891 a chair, in its history at the Sorbonne. How novel this was is attested to by the fact that its first occupant, who became the first academic embodiment of the Revolution, was not even a historian by formation. Alphonse Aulard (1849–1928) was a student of Italian literature and an expert on the great romantic poet Leopardi, who became a historian of the Revolution because he was a committed Republican.

So we have to remember that in 1889 the academic historiography of the Revolution was in its infancy. Acton, who knew the international historiographical literature better than most, listed only three men whom he described as "modern historians" in his 1895 lectures: Sybel, Taine, and Sorel; and two of these wrote primarily about the international aspects of the Revolution.[28] But this was soon to change. By 1914 Aulard's successors in the Sorbonne chair were already adults, and indeed, until the end of the 1950s, the history of the Revolution remained dominated by the long-lived generation that had come to maturity by 1900: Mathiez and Lefebvre were born in 1874, Sagnac in 1868, and Caron in 1875. (Aulard himself was born in 1849.) With the exception of Georges Lefebvre, exiled in provincial high schools, the new generation had already published extensively and was established—and Lefebvre, who only had a local monograph to his credit, had virtually completed research on his great thesis on the peasants of the *Nord* department and the Revolution, which was to be published in 1924.

Contrary to what is now often claimed, none of these historians was a Marxist. (Indeed, not even the Russians who pioneered the study of the agrarian question in France during this period, and stimulated Lefebvre, were Marxists: I.V. Luchitskii [1845–1918] and N.I. Kareiev [1850–1931] were both Liberals, although the latter originally had populist links.) Mathiez claimed to be a socialist, but the general consensus among his contemporaries was that he was basically a man of 1793.[29] Lefebvre, a socialist from the industrial North, was more deeply imbued with the ideas of the labour movement, and certainly impressed with Marx's materialist conception of history, but his real master was Jaurès, who married some of Marx—too little, and wrongly understood, the Marxists of his day might say—with a good deal of Michelet. The historians of the French Revolution were impassioned, democratic Republicans of the Jacobin persuasion, and this automatically pushed them to a position on the left edge of the political spectrum. For, was it not Aulard himself, a man very far from extremism, who thought that logically the French Revolution led to socialism, although only a minority of Frenchmen realised it?[30] It is not absolutely clear what he or most other politicians calling themselves socialists in France around 1900 meant by the word, but it was unquestionably a badge signalling one's position on the side of progress, the people, and the Left. And it is hardly an accident that so many of the makers of the classical historiography of the Revolution came from that temple of the Republic, which knew no enemies on the Left, the stronghold of Dreyfusards, the *Ecole Normale Supérieure* of the rue d'Ulm: Aulard himself,

Sagnac, Mathiez, Jean Jaurès—although also, it must be said, in an earlier generation, Taine.

Let us take a brief and necessarily impressionistic, quantitative look at the historiography of the Revolution since the first centenary.[31] On a rough estimate the British Museum (British Library) added more than 150 titles every five years in 1881–1900, more than 250 in 1901–1905, more than 330 in 1906–1910, and —to date—an all-time maximum of approximately 450 titles in 1911–1915.[32] The first postwar era kept up a steady level of 150–175 every five years, but the second half of the 1930s—the Popular Front era—saw a distinct rise to 225, which is not reflected in the reviewing of the *Times Literary Supplement,* unlike the pre-1914 boom. After a modest start in the second postwar era, the 1960s and 1970s record a striking take-off: nearly 300 in the second half of the 1960s. This is clearly reflected in the *TLS* for the 1970s. We may take it that the 1980s will probably record a greater boom than that before 1914—a natural accompaniment to the second centenary, and to modern media and editorial publicity.

Yet, although quantity may indicate the general level of interest in the Revolution, in itself it tells us little about its nature. Here a glance at the biographical side of this literature may be helpful. Before World War I this is dominated by works on the French royal family—Marie Antoinette and the rest—that fill columns of bibliography, and, it must be presumed, appealed primarily to conservative and counter-revolutionary readers. Since World War I, this branch of revolutionary historiography has faded away, and is today insignificant. On the other hand, the studies of individual revolutionary personalities or leaders and their works were written by authors of varying political attitudes and at varying levels of seriousness, ranging from salon entertainment to heavyweight scholarship. This makes the variations in interest in particular figures instructive. Thus, the most moderate of the leading figures, Mirabeau, clearly had his peak before 1914, after which interest in him dropped sharply. Except for a blip in the 1960s and again in the 1980s, he has aroused no interest since World War II—even though a man who was not only a leading figure in the Revolution but also an economist of distinction, not to mention a pornographer, might be expected to attract authors.[33] The centrist Danton, less prominent, had his peak in the 1920s, with some action in the 1900s and 1930s and—as we have seen—around the time of the first centenary. Robespierre was not particularly prominent until the 1900s—he ran more or less level with Marat as representative of radical Jacobinism until the mid-1900s, but, since then, he has attracted more attention than any other figure—although part of this is not so much biographical as a reflection of his role in the Jacobin Republic. However, the peak periods for this figure are, perhaps not surprisingly, the second half of the 1930s—the Popular Front era—and the 1960s and 1970s. On the extreme left Marat has increasingly been replaced as a flag-carrier by Saint-Just, although a certain interest in him seems to have been maintained from the days of the October Revolution in the Soviet Union.[34] Apart from Vellay's edition of Saint-Just's writings in 1908, the British Library records nothing by or about him before World War I (as against 11 titles on Marat). Interest—no longer adequately reflected in the British Library—became noticeable in the 1930s, but—as one might expect of a figure who, unlike Marat, appeals primarily to intellectuals—it reached a modest peak in the 1970s and 1980s. On the extreme left Babeuf, the first Communist, is nowhere before World War I, and makes an appearance in the 1930s. His period of maximum prominence is in the 1960s (which celebrated the bicentenary of his birth) and the 1970s. What this suggests is that the maximum of a specifically leftwing interest in the historiography of the Revolution is found in the 1930s and again the 1960s and 1970s. In both cases we have the combination of a strong Communist party and a more general radicalisation. It is against this that we must situate the reaction, which was political rather than historiographical after 1940 (Georges

Lefebvre's *Quatre-Vingt-Neuf* was confiscated by Vichy as subversive), but is both political and historiographical today.[35]

Let us take a rapid look at the serious historiographical production. Here we can distinguish five periods. During all of these, except the last and present one, the leading French historiography of the subject was passionately Republican and Jacobin. The antirevolutionaries had no serious scholarly standing, although a good many readers. Only one of them has been a candidate for rehabilitation, namely Auguste Cochin (1876–1916), a defender of Taine against the onslaught of Aulard, whom François Furet (not a *Normalien*) has taken up. The classical Third Republic Radical and Radical-Socialist version, political and institutional, coincides with the era of Aulard. As has already been suggested, during this period from the 1880s to the First World War, the foundations of modern scholarly historiography were laid. After World War I, the field in France moves to the left, and becomes markedly socialist—Aulard was in decline well before his death in 1928—although again French socialist and communist historians remain committed to the Jacobins, especially Robespierre, and not to the ancestors of their own movement; and not even to the Lenin of 1917, who, of all the revolutionaries, singled out Danton for praise as "the greatest master of revolutionary tactics yet known."[36] The 1920s were dominated by Mathiez, who, incidentally, underlined his socialist convictions by reediting Jaurès *Histoire Socialiste de la Révolution Française*, which had originally been published under political rather than academic auspices. Although he never got *the* chair, he dominated the *Société des Etudes Robespierristes*, and through it the field. Mathiez's version became the most influential. Rapidly taken up in the United States, where, perhaps because of the republican tradition, interest in the history of the French Revolution was well established in the universities—Harvard actually bought Aulard's library— his synthesis of revolutionary history was soon translated and a shorthand version of it included in the Seligman *Encyclopedia of the Social Sciences* in the early 1930s, where it may still be profitably consulted.

I will not dwell on Mathiez's bitter hostility to Danton, which divided him from Aulard even before the First World War, since it is chiefly of local French interest; in any case, one may suspect that it largely reflected Mathiez's oedipal feelings for the founder of the field, whom he failed to succeed in the Sorbonne chair.

Aulard was succeeded in the chair by Philippe Sagnac, a central figure in French positivist historiography, but not a man who imparted a special profile to his position. However, *de facto* Mathiez succeeded Aulard and his successor was Georges Lefebvre (1874–1959) who, in 1932, took his place as the chairman of the *Société des Etudes Robespierristes* and director of Mathiez's *Annales Historiques de la Révolution Française*, which had long replaced Aulard's fading journal *La Révolution Française* as the organ of revolutionary historiography. Lefebvre, who dominated the 1930s—and indeed the entire period until his death—had been a very slow starter, perhaps because he lacked the backing of an elite institution. Exiled in the secondary schools of the North—he is said to have been the only active supporter of Dreyfus in Boulogne-sur-mer—he was not even able to concentrate on the French Revolution, for his university patron in provincial Lille prevailed on him to translate a then standard work, Stubbs's *Constitutional History of England*, in three volumes, to which he added a supplement in the 1920s. This implausible excursion into English medieval history, made even more implausible by the fact that the original author of that Victorian classic had been a bishop, had the minor advantage of making English historians quicker to appreciate Lefebvre than American ones. The only time in his life that he left France was for an academic visit to England in 1934. It is quite possible that Lefebvre spent nights in Britain before he ever—at the age of sixty—spent a night in Paris. After the publication of his great and ground-breaking work on the peasantry, he was able to occupy a university chair: first in Clermont-Ferrand—at the time, the academic Siberia of France—then in Strasbourg, unusually open to talent since its return to France after the war, and the base from which Marc Bloch and Lucien Febvre launched their attack on historical orthodoxy in the *Annales*, and prepared to capture Paris. To Paris Lefebvre also came in 1935, finally moving to the canonical Chair in the History of the Revolution upon Sagnac's retirement in 1937.

Slow though his start had been, Lefebvre made up for lost time. The 1930s were dominated by a number of classic volumes: the 1932 study of *The Great Fear of 1789*, which is the starting point for most of today's "history from below" (a term coined by Lefebvre); the superb history of Europe in the Napoleonic Era (1935), superior to the preceding volume on the French Revolution in the same series written only partly by him (but later revised); the continuation of Mathiez's three volumes into the era of Thermidor—Lefebvre did not publish the final volume on the Directory until 1946; and, above all, the most impressive monument anyone was to erect on the one hundred and fiftieth anniversary of the Revolution in 1939, a little book simply called *Quatre-Vingt Neuf (Eighty-nine)* in French, but familiar to all under R.R. Palmer's title and 1947 translation, *The Coming of the French Revolution*. It was the tribute by the French Popular Front in its dying days to the Revolution it could no longer adequately commemorate. This book is essentially what modern revisionist historiography is attacking; but not without respect. For Lefebvre, whether we agree with him or not, was a very great historian. In the opinion of this writer, and even of Lefebvre's adversaries, he was by far the most impressive modern historian of the Revolution. Politically he was a Socialist at the time he wrote his major works, but after the war he sympathised with the Communists.

Two other historiographical observations may be made about the 1930s. First, they seem so completely dominated by Lefebvre, chiefly because another great historian of the French

Revolution is, or became, chiefly known as an economic and social historian: Ernest Labrousse (1895–1988), who died in his nineties. Labrousse was another of the committed intellectuals of the Left who took to history, although he was more active in politics than most. After a brief period in the Communist party in the early 1920s following the Congress of Tours, when a majority of Socialists split away, he rejoined the Socialist party and became Chef de Cabinet to Leon Blum for a while. His major work on the Revolution was a massive study of the economic crisis of the *ancien régime* in the second half of the 1780s. He explained the origin of the Revolution in terms of a coincidence of a major economic and political crisis in the old system, and later wrote a paper ("How Revolutions Are Born")[37] that attempted to generalise this somewhat mechanical model for 1830 and 1848. Labrousse belongs, by biography and spirit, to the Third Republic and its tradition, but, unlike other historians, he did consider himself a Marxist, although very much in the old-fashioned, economic-determinist or Kautskyan mode. Braudel considered him the only other major French historian and regretted—or pretended to regret—that French history suffered because he and Labrousse did not get along. The other point to make about the 1930s is that they saw the launching of modern scholarship on revolutionary history in the United States (where the field was already established) and in Britain. Both are or became the main non-French centres for this research.

The postwar period, until the middle 1960s—Lefebvre died in 1959—was dominated by Lefebvre and his pupils who, by then, were much more closely associated with the Communist party; although his successor (after an interval of Marcel Reinhard [1899–1973]), Albert Soboul (1914–1982) was just as typical a figure of the Republican tradition as any of his predecessors: there are marvellous obituaries of both Lefebvre and Soboul by Richard Cobb, pupil of the one and friend of the other, although about as far removed from Marxism as possible, except for being a historian fascinated by the

anonymous people at the grass roots of history, and therefore
drawn to the only historians who practised the history of the
common people in the Revolution, Lefebvre and his communist
following. One notes in passing that the brilliant group of
younger historians who left the Communist party in the middle
1950s after a phase of rigid Stalinsim—the most eminent of
them, Emmanuel Le Roy Ladurie, has described his politico-
educational progress[38]—had shown very little interest in the
French Revolution, being much more attracted to the *Annales*
school; however, two ex-Communists, François Furet and Denis
Richet, inaugurated the revisionist wave in France. Since
Albert Soboul's untimely death in 1982, the Sorbonne chair
has been occupied by Michel Vovelle (born 1933) another
Communist, but one whose original research was in the field
of cultural history or the history of "mentalities," which
exercised a strong and beneficent attraction on several
talented leftwing historians in the 1960s and 1970s.

However, since the war it has no longer been possible to
think of French Revolution historiography as primarily
French. Lefebvre's own pupils were an international group,
and the number of Ph.D.s in the subject in Britain took off
vertically in the 1950s and 1960s. There had been no theses
before 1910, about six per decade thereafter until 1950—
actually nine in the 1930s—but then, in the 1950s eighteen
and in the 1960s twenty.[39]

Let me now take a brief look at the significance of these
phases of the interpretation of the Revolution. In France it
reflected the history of the Third Republic while that regime
lasted—that is, until 1940. That is to say, the formation of the
major school of French Revolutionary historians reflects the
institutionalisation of the Third Republic as a democracy that
referred back to the Revolution as its founding experience.
The great outburst of revolutionary historiography in the
1900s, I suggest, reflected the triumph of the Republic over the
many crises of its infancy—culminating in the Dreyfus Affair,
a triumph ratified by the separation of Church and State, and

the emergence of the Radical Socialists as the central party of the Republic. They were, as we all know, neither radical nor socialist, but were profoundly committed to the Republic and therefore the Revolution, and several of their leading politicians, notably the chubby and gastronomically minded intellectual Edouard Herriot (1872–1957) between the wars (also a *Normalien*), were quite serious practising historians of the revolutionary period. Herriot published a volume of speeches called *Homage to the Revolution* in the year of its 150th anniversary—despite the fact that the Jacobin Terror had done its best to raze his hometown and political base, the great city of Lyon, on grounds of counterrevolutionary activity. (He had also written a history of this.)[40] The triumph of the Republic over its enemies, as the Dreyfus affair had demonstrated, was based on an alliance of the centre with the Left—even the extreme Left. The basic political principle of Third Republicanism was consequently: "No enemies on the left," and therefore no rejection of the heritage of the Jacobin Republic. Although Robespierre and Saint-Just, let alone Marat, aroused enthusiasm only on the far left, even moderates went for Danton who had been both a Jacobin, and an opponent of Robespierre, and of the excesses of The Terror. Louis Barthou, a moderate Republican politician best known by his death—he was assassinated with King Alexander of Yugoslavia in 1934 by a Yugoslav terrorist—wrote biographies of both Mirabeau and Danton, and also a book on the Ninth Thermidor, that is, the fall of Robespierre. This, I suggest, is also the key to Aulard's idealisation of Danton.

After the 1900s one has the impression that for a while the Revolution became for mainstream Republicans a matter of 14th of July oratory rather than of major ideological urgency. The centre of gravity of revolutionary historiography moved to the left: not so much in political terms as in social terms. It is not insignificant, in my view, that the major work of Aulard's successor as chief of revolutionary history, was about food prices and social unrest in the era of The Terror, although

Mathiez had first published on religious history; or that Mathiez's successor, Lefebvre, wrote his thesis on the peasantry of the North in the Revolution; or that *his* successor Soboul's magnum opus dealt with the Parisian sansculottes— that is, with the rank-and-file grass-roots activists. (Incidentally, none of these historians idealised his subjects: Mathiez and Soboul were firmly on the side of Robespierre against his leftwing opponents, and Lefebvre saw his peasants without illusions, or rather in the perspective of the urban Jacobins.)[41] More generally, the history of the Revolution increasingly shifts into a social and economic key. I have already mentioned Labrousse, but, to take other examples among the older generation of experts in the field, Marcel Reinhard was one of the first to go into the demographic history of the revolutionary period, although he also—a little later— published the standard biography of the Jacobin military organiser, Carnot.[42] Jacques Godechot (born 1907), president of the *Société des Etudes Robespierristes*, although primarily interested in institutional and general history, also found himself drawn into demography. Initially this almost certainly reflected not Marxism—for the Marxist tradition in France was negligible—but the rise of the socialist and labour movement: if you like, the influence of Jaurès. However, it helped to shift revolutionary historiography closer to common ground with the Marxists who had previously been the chief school interested in the economic and social dimensions of history. In the 1930s this convergence was reinforced by a crucial development: the rise of international fascism, which drew most other schools of reactionary, traditionalist and rightwing conservative politics into its wake.

This development was crucial, because fascism was the quintessential expression of those who had, from the start, rejected the Revolution completely. Indeed, until the middle twentieth century, the extreme Right could almost be defined by its rejection of the Revolution, that is, not only of Jacobinism and all its political progeny, but of liberalism, and the entire ideology of the eighteenth-century Enlightenment and nineteeth-century progress, not to mention the emancipation of the Jews, which had been one of the most signal achievements of the Revolution. There was no question where the French Right stood: it wanted to reverse the French Revolution, even though most of it did not really believe in the restoration of the Bourbon monarchy, which its most active militants in the *Action Française* demanded. The only time the French Right actually overthrew the Republic, in 1940–1944, it kept monarchism out of sight, even though its ideological influence on the men of Vichy was very noticeable, merely establishing an otherwise undefined and authoritarian "French State." There was no doubt where the Catholic Church in the time of Vatican I stood. It did not expect to abolish 1789 everywhere—although it did in Spain under Franco, Freemasons and all—but it would have wanted to. And there was no doubt at all where fascism stood. Mussolini said so himself in his article on fascism in his Italian Encyclopedia. He stood "against the feeble and materialist positivism of the nineteenth century.... against all the individualist abstractions of the eighteenth century kind, and.... against all utopias and Jacobin innovations."[43] The same was even more obviously true in Germany, where the national ideology had long been suspicious not only of western liberalism but of the French as immoralists, nationalists, and Germany's so-called hereditary enemy.

Inevitably, therefore, in the 1930s all antifascists tended to rally round the French Revolution, which was the main target of their enemies. One might say that rallying round the memory of the French Revolution was ideologically what the Popular Front was politically: the union of all antifascists. It was no accident that the French labour unions after 1936 financed Jean Renoir to make a film on *La Marseillaise*, or, as I myself remember, an elaborate theatrical production of Romain Rolland's rather boring *Quatorze Juillet* was performed in Paris in the summer of 1936. But there was

87

another reason why the Popular Front developed a cult of *Marseillaise*, tricolour, and the Jacobins of 1793–1794. They were the original French patriots, the saviours of France in a war of national—and ideological—defence against the local reactionaries who went abroad and allied themselves with their country's enemies.

For reasons that need not concern us here, in the last two decades of the nineteenth century, the vocabulary of French patriotism and nationalism had passed from the Left to the Right.[44] Again, for reasons that I cannot consider here, the socialist and proletarian Left during that period had reacted to the cooptation of *Marseillaise* tricolour, and the rest by the official Third Republic, by turning away from the patriotic, warlike side of the Jacobin tradition. It became associated with antimilitarism, even with pacifism. Chiefly under Communist party influence it now reached out once again for the symbols of national patriotism, not unconscious of the fact that the *Marseillaise* and the Jacobin tricolour were also symbols of radical social revolution. Antifascism and, later, the Resistance to German occupation, were both patriotic and committed to social transformation. The Communist party looked as though it would succeed in taking over the traditions of the Republic: it was one of the things De Gaulle worried about in the Resistance years.

As it happened, the recuperation of Jacobin patriotism was a good move ideologically, for the weakness of rightwing French historiography had always been that it could not quite reject an episode as glorious and triumphant in the history of France as the victories and conquests of the revolutionary and Napoleonic era. The rightwing historians who wrote elegant and intelligent popularisations were united in singing the praises of the old regime and in denouncing Robespierre. Yet, how could even they dismiss those glorious military feats of French soldiers, especially when achieved against Prussians and English? All this meant that the historiography of the French Revolution became both more leftwing and more

Jacobin. Politically the Popular Front broke down. Historiographically it produced its greatest triumph in 1939 as war drew near: Georges Lefebvre's *The Coming of the French Revolution.* And if for the next generation it dominated the field, it was in memory of Resistance and Liberation as much as of the Third Republic.

By this time, the fusion of the Republican, Jacobin, Socialist, and Communist traditions was pretty complete, for the Popular Front and later the Resistance turned the Communist party into the major party on the left; and in the 1930s we can actually begin to trace the direct influence of Marxism in the French Left. But what exactly was that influence in terms of the Great Revolution? Marx himself never analysed it as a historian, as he did the 1848 Revolution in France, the Second Republic, and the Paris Commune. Even Engels, always more drawn to historical writing, never produced a coherent version even as a popular sketch. As we have seen, the idea of the Revolution as the bourgeois victory in the class struggle, which Marx took over, came from the Restoration bourgeois Liberals. Marxism welcomed the idea of the Revolution as a people's revolution and tried to look at it from the grass-roots perspective, but this was even less specifically Marxist: it belonged to Michelet. The idealisation of The Terror and of Robespierre goes back to the Babouvists, and especially Buonarroti, who transposed the radical Revolution of 1793–1794 into the key of nineteenth-century proletarian communism. However, although Babeuf was admired as an early Communist, he was certainly no more likely to appeal theoretically to Marx than Weitling or Thomas Spence, and the cult of Robespierre was in no sense Marxist. Indeed, as we have seen, what became the mainstream Marxist tradition chose to align itself with Robespierre against the ultraradicals who opposed him from the left, a choice that is comprehensible only on the assumption that Marxists took over the Jacobin tradition rather than the other way round. In itself it seems as surprising for modern Communists to champion Robespierre against Hébert and Jacques Roux, as it would be for British Socialists and Communists, with all their admiration for regicides and republic in the seventeenth century, to champion Cromwell against the Levellers and Diggers. As a matter of fact, Marxist historians committed to *both* the concept of the Revolution as a bourgeois revolution *and* to the Jacobin Republic as the embodiment of its more advanced achievements, have had considerable trouble in deciding exactly who represented the bourgeoisie in the era of the Committee of Public Safety, which was about as fond of businessmen as William Jennings Bryan was of Eastern bankers. Incidentally, neither Engels nor Marx took so simple-minded a view of the Jacobin Republic.

Certainly the Jacobin interpretation of the Revolution had been to some extent "Marxianised," by Jaurès and his successors, but chiefly in the sense that they paid more attention than their predecessors to the social and economic factors in its origin and progress, and particularly in the mobilisation of its popular component. In the broadest sense, the post-Jaurès interpretation of the Revolution as bourgeois, did not advance significantly beyond the Liberal thesis of an upheaval that ratified the long historical rise of the bourgeoisie, by 1789 ready to replace feudalism. The Marxists remained within the limits of the Jacobin interpretation in this respect also. The well-known articles on "non-capitalist wealth" by George V. Taylor, which, more than Cobban, form the real starting point for revisionism, were not so much critiques of Marxist or Jacobin researches on the subject, which hardly existed, as demonstrations that it was not enough to *assume* that a bourgeoisie had arisen, but the term had to be defined and the rise demonstrated.[45]

In short, the Marxists took far more from the Republican historiography of the Revolution as it developed in the twentieth century than they contributed to it. However, there is no doubt that they made that historiography their own, and hence ensured that an attack on Marxism would also be an attack on it.

Surviving Revision

What we have seen in the past twenty years or so is a massive historiographical reaction against this canonical view. Twenty years ago, Lefebvre was praised in extravagant terms by John McManners in the *New Cambridge Modern History* and his synthesis was said to hold the field. Crane Brinton, hardly a standard-bearer of Leninism, basically dismissed Alfred Cobban's *Social Interpretation of the French Revolution*, the cornerstone of modern revisionism, as the work of an old-fashioned, antitheoretical historian who, since even someone such as he cannot do without an "interpretation," comes up with something much more simple-minded than what he rejects.[1] But, in 1989, an excellent and balanced book based on the old view, George Rudé's *The French Revolution* (1988), was dismissed as the work of a man who "is worrying about the distribution of the cargo when the ship that was torpedoed ... is at the bottom of the sea" and as "a recapitulation of old ideas that are no longer credible in the light of recent research. It no longer fits the facts as they are perceived today."[2] And a French historian describes the work of François Furet as "diffuser les thèses de Cobban et de ses successeurs" ("give currency to the theses of Cobban and his followers").[3] I doubt if any previous period of French revolutionary historiography has seen as dramatic a reversal of judgements as these.

The sheer extremism of some current statements should warn us that we are dealing with more than purely academic emotions. So should the words "the facts as they are *perceived* today" (emphasis added), which means not the facts but our interpretation of them. This is confirmed by the attempts to show that the French Revolution was in some sense *unimportant*, which is not only implausible, but runs counter to the universal opinion of the nineteenth century. In short, that it was the very opposite of the inevitable social change that the young Benjamin Constant, first and most moderate of the great moderate bourgeois Liberals, had in mind when he wrote in 1796: "We must, in the end, yield to the necessity which sweeps us along, we must cease to ignore the march of society."[4] It was—I cite a recent opinion—"haphazard in its origins and ineffectual in its outcome."[5] There are indeed ideologists, some of them historians, who write as if the Revolution can be written out of the script of modern history, leaving the basic storyline unaffected—although the author of the last quotation is not among them. The absurdity of the assumption that the French Revolution is simply a sort of stumble on the long, slow march of eternal France, is patent.

The official justification for this reversal is said to be the accumulation of research that has made old views untenable. There has indeed been a striking growth of research in this field, although not so much in France, and certainly not among revisionists in that country. Paradoxically, the ranking postwar historiographical orthodoxy, the *Annales* school (insofar as it was a school) took little interest in what was regarded as the superficial phenomena of the history of events such as politics, including revolutions. This is perhaps one reason why the history of the Revolution was left largely to the Marxists, who believed that revolutions are important historical events. What most French revisionists are doing is, to quote the title of François Furet's book, *Interpreting the French Revolution (Penser la Révolution Française*), that is, fitting the known facts together differently. Such new facts as have come into circulation are largely due to American and British researchers. On six reference pages of a recent revisionist work, chosen at random, I find eighty-nine references to foreign works and fifty-one to French works.[6] Given the national pride of French scholars and the centrality of the Revolution to their national history, one may suspect that ideological inclination may have helped to make some of them so readily receptive to foreigners' opinions. In any case, the beginnings of revisionism go back to a time before all this new research was available, namely to Alfred Cobban's (1901–1968) attack on the concept of the Revolution as a bourgeois revolution in 1955.[7] In short, the argument has not been about facts but about interpretations.

One might go even further. It has not been so much about the French Revolution as about what broad historiographical and political generalisations can be read into it. A historiographically uncommitted reader—for example, a well-read sociologist—can point out, time and again, that on the facts of the situation there is actually very little disagreement between the revisionists and the best of the old scholarship,[8] although the outline histories of the late Albert Soboul (but not his outstanding work on the Parisian sansculottes) sometimes leaves itself open to Furet's jibes about "une sorte de vulgate lenino-populiste."[9] If Georges Lefebvre had published his works not in the 1920s and 1930s but, as an unknown researcher, in the 1960s and 1970s, they would hardly have been read as the pillars of an orthodoxy that must today be controverted. They would have been read as a contribution to its revision.[10]

An example may illustrate this. One of the major revisionist arguments against considering the French Revolution a bourgeois revolution is that such a revolution, on Marxist assumptions, should, by rights, have advanced capitalism in France, whereas it is evident that the French economy did not do particularly well during and after the revolutionary era ("Le mythe marxiste assimilant la Révolution à une étape décisive dans le développement de l'économie capitaliste est facilement démentie par la stagnation de l'économie pendant la période révolutionnaire et au delà").[11] If anything, nineteenth-century economic development in France lagged behind that of several other countries. The first fact was already well known to Frederick Engels, who commented on it without any apparent sense that it was supposed to invalidate his views.[12] The second was generally accepted by most economic historians of the first half of this century, including Marxists. The large body of literature on French "economic retardation," attests to this—although more modern work has encouraged revision-ism in this field also. However, Georges Lefebvre not only took the negative effect of the Revolution on the subsequent development of French capitalism for granted, but specifically tried to explain it by analysing the agrarian settlement of the Revolution. Similar explanations were taken up even by the flag-carrier of the bourgeois revolution orthodoxy, Albert Soboul, to account for the relative backwardness of French compared to British capitalism.[13] Both may be legitimately criticised, but not for failing to observe or take account of what seems so evident to their critics. Arguments about interpreta-tion are of a different order from arguments about fact.

This is not, of course, to deny that research on the Revolu-tion has advanced quite spectacularly since the Second World War—probably more so than at any period since the quarter-century preceding 1914—and that its historiography therefore requires broadening, updating, revision, or other modific-ations to take account of new questions, new answers, and new data. This is most obviously the case for the period leading up to the Revolution. Thus, Lefebvre's "aristocratic reaction, steadily taking shape and growing from the end of Louis xiv's reign, and which is the most important feature of French history in the eighteenth century" has not survived well, and it is at present hard to see anyone trying to revive it.[14] More generally, revolutionary history must henceforth take far more account of the regions and groups in French society most neglected in the traditional and politically oriented historiography: notably women, the "unpolitical" parts of the French people, and the counterrevolutionaries. It is not quite so clear that it ought to take as much account as some historians do, of contemporary fashions of analysis—history as "rhetoric," revolution as symbolism, deconstruction, and the like.

It is equally undeniable that traditional French Republican historiography, both before and since its convergence and interpenetration with the Marxist version, tended to become both a pedagogic and an ideological orthodoxy, highly resistant to change. To take a relatively minor example. In the 1950s the suggestion by R.R. Palmer and Jacques Godechot that the French Revolution was part of a wider Atlantic movement against the western old regimes,[15] met with indignant opposition in Marxist historical circles, although the idea was suggestive and interesting, and both authors belonged to the mainstream of revolutionary historiography.[16] The objections were essentially political. On the one hand, Communists in the 1950s were deeply suspicious of the term *Atlantic*, since it seemed designed to reinforce the western contention that the United States and western Europe belonged together against eastern Europe (as in *North Atlantic Treaty Organisation*). This objection to Atlanticism in history as a political term unwisely introduced into an academic field was, incidentally, shared by scholars of unblemished conservatism.[17] On the other hand, the suggestion that the French Revolution was not a unique and, historically speaking, uniquely decisive, phenomenon, seemed to weaken the uniqueness and world-decisiveness of the "great" revolutions then and later, not to mention the national pride of Frenchmen, especially revolutionary Frenchmen. If orthodoxies were so sensitive to relatively minor modifications, then their resistance to major challenges was likely to be far greater.

However, challenges to ideological or political interpretations must not be confused with historical revisions, even though the two cannot always be clearly separated, especially in so explosively political a field as the history of the French Revolution. Yet, when we consider the current challenge, insofar as it is political and ideological, there is a curious disproportion between the passions involved and the targets at which they are directed. For, just as the extension of political democracy in western parliamentary societies was the shadow that loomed over the debates on the occasion of the first centenary of 1789, so, too, the Russian Revolution and its successors loomed over the ideological debates on the occasion of its second bicentenary. The only people who still attack 1789 as such are old-fashioned French conservatives and the heirs of that Right which always defined itself by the rejection of all the Enlightenment stood for. There are, of course, still plenty of those. The Liberal revision of French Revolutionary history is entirely directed, *via* 1789, at 1917. It is an irony of history that, in doing so, it attacks, as we have seen in the first chapter, precisely that interpretation of the Revolution that was first formulated and popularised by the very school of moderate liberalism of which they see themselves as the heirs.

Hence, the wild use of such terms as *gulag* (very much a buzzword in French intellectual circles since Solzhenitsyn), of the Orwellspeak of *1984*, the references to totalitarianism, the stress on agitators and ideologists as the makers of 1789, and the insistence on the Jacobins as the ancestors of the vanguard party (Furet, updating Cochin). Hence the insistence on the de Tocqueville who saw continuities in history as against the de Tocqueville who saw the Revolution as the creator of a "new society."[18] Hence, also, the preference for the old Guizot who claimed that people like him "rejected both assertions: they refused both the return to the maxims of the Old Regime and any even speculative adherence to the revolutionary principles,[19] over the young Guizot who had written in 1820:

I will still say the Revolution, brought on by the necessary development of a society in progress, founded on moral principles, undertaken with the design of the general good, was the *terrible* but *legitimate* battle of right against privilege, of legal liberty against despotism, and that to the Revolution alone belongs the task of regulating itself, of purging itself, of founding the constitutional monarchy to consummate the good that it had begun and to repair the evil that it had done.[20]

Hence, in short, the general line of argument in favour of gradual reform and change over revolution and the specific line of argument that the French Revolution had not made all that much of a difference to the evolution of France and what difference it had made had been achieved at more cost than it was worth.[21]

In fact, the assumption that the French Revolution achieved nothing commensurate with its costs, is essential to histories of it written as contemporary political denunciations, like Simon Schama's exceptionally stylish and eloquent bestseller *Citizens*, since it leaves the author free to concentrate on what can be presented as gratuitous horror and suffering. No doubt in due course someone who can no longer recognise what the Second World War was fought about, at least in Europe, will write a marvellously talented and embittered history of it, which will see it as a pointless and probably avoidable catastrophe that caused far more death and destruction in Europe than the First World War, and achieved little that would not otherwise have happened. It is, of course, easier to view such events from an uncomprehending distance, if they are sufficiently remote for involvement to be optional. Schama is not involved as an expert in the field; for, although extremely well-read, his book does not set out to add to the knowledge already available. The author's choice of a narrative focused on particular people and incidents, neatly sidesteps the problems of perspective and generalisation. And, writing one hundred and fifty years after Carlyle, whose technique of the brilliant set-piece story he takes up again, Schama no longer feels himself part of the drama, as Carlyle did, but merely a disenchanted chronicler of the crimes and follies of mankind.

Nevertheless, although it is quite natural for Liberal intellectuals to use the experience of the French Revolution as an argument against modern communist revolutions, and, conversely, to look critically at Robespierre in the light of Stalin or Mao—as indeed Soviet historians themselves are now doing—to the naked eye the dangers of social revolution of the Russian or Chinese, or, if we prefer, Cambodian or *Sendero Luminoso* Peruvian type, seem rather remote in the developed countries of the 1980s, not least in France—more remote, indeed, than the possible dangers of democracy seemed in 1889. It is natural for historians who have lived through the experience of far greater atrocities than those of 1793–1794 to bring this experience to bear on the 1790s, just as it was natural for British historians who had lived through the Second World War to reconsider The Terror of the Year II as perhaps the first example of the planned total war mobilisation which they had recently experienced. However, why should anyone except those who have always rejected 1789, insist on the French Revolution as an example of what can happen when revolutions are not avoided or present maximal estimates of the losses and disruptions it brought to France— which no serious historian has tried to conceal—when, among the actual dangers to the social fabric of France, or of all modern urbanised societies, those presented by the successors to Robespierre and Saint-Just are probably by far the most negligible? There is a notable disproportion between the mere fact of the bicentenary in a relatively stable western world and the passions to which it seemingly gave rise in France, although it must be said that elsewhere the occasion was commemorated in a less contentious spirit.

What was explosive in the France of 1989 was not the state of the country, but the passions of its intellectuals, especially those whose high profile in the increasingly important media of opinion, had given them unusual prominence.[22] The revisionist attack on the Revolution reflected not an apprehended danger of social upheaval, but a settling of accounts on the Left Bank of Paris. Mainly a settling of accounts with the writers' own pasts, that is to say with that Marxism which had, as Raymond Aron noted, been the general foundation of the changing ideological fashions that had dominated the Parisian intellectual scene for thirty years after Liberation.[23] The details of this chapter of French intellectual history need not concern us here. Its origins go back to the period of fascism, or rather antifascism, when the traditional ideology of the Enlightenment and Republican values—of the belief in reason, science, progress, and the Rights of Man—found itself converging with communism at the very moment when it became firmly and ruthlessly Stalinist—not least in the homegrown Communist party of France, which therefore, between 1935 and 1945, became virtually coterminous with the native Jacobin tradition, and the largest political organisation in the country.

Certainly not all French intellectuals of the Left were, or became, members of the Communist party, although the number among the students who did in postwar France, especially in some elite institutions, was impressive: during the first Cold War something like a quarter of all students at the Ecole Normale Supérieure of the rue d'Ulm, admittedly an establishment with traditions of the Republican Left, carried PCF cards.[24] (Before the war the Latin Quarter had been dominated rather by students of the ultraright.) Nevertheless, whether intellectuals were or had been in the party or not, it remains true that "from the Liberation until 1981, the PCF exercised a serpentine fascination over the radical intelligentsia of France" because it represented the mass basis of the Left—indeed, with the decline of the old Socialist party before its reconstitution on a new base by Mitterrand, virtually the only political representative of the Left.[25] Moreover, since virtually all governments from the end of antifascist unity (1947) to the 1980s were, with momentary exceptions, based on centre and (Gaullist) right, intellectuals were rarely tempted to abandon a posture of left opposition. A serious rethinking of the political perspectives of the Left, which the European experiences of the 1950s and 1960s might have suggested, could be postponed until after Gaullism, and, for a brief moment of rebel rhetoric and illusion—at the end of the 1960s, it did not even seem necessary. The retirement of the General and the end of the illusions of 1968, also marked the end of the era of *marxisant* intellectual hegemony. The backlash in France was all the more dramatic, because the gap between abstract high theory and the social reality to which it was somehow supposed to relate, had become almost unbridgeable—except by the spiderwebs of philosophical subtlety that could bear no weights. In any case, intellectual fashion dictates the ideological colours to be worn during the current cycle, as *haute couture* dictates the season's colours. Soon Marxists were harder to find than old-style positivists, or the ones that survived were dismissed as old hat. Even before his death, Jean-Paul Sartre had become someone not to be bothered with. When, after his death, an American publisher wished to buy the rights to the biography which he naturally supposed to be in preparation, he discovered that no French publisher had thought it worth commissioning such a work.* Sartre had disappeared from sight in the Fifth Arrondissement, although the success of Annie Cohen-Solal's biography in France and a number of other countries demonstrated that the name still meant a great deal to a broader public.

This crisis of French Marxism affected the French Revolution for general and specific reasons. In general terms, the Revolution, and especially Jacobinism, was, as we have seen, the image in which the French Left had been formed. Specifically, as Tony Judt has persuasively argued, French revolutionary history in a real sense *replaces* much of political theory or enquiry on the French Left.[26] The rejection of old radical

---

*In fact, an author was found, the book was commissioned (in French) from New York and the rights sold to the French.

beliefs therefore automatically implies a revisionist attack on the history of the Revolution. Only, as Judt has not failed to note, this is not an attack on a Marxist interpretation, but on what French radical intellectuals have been doing since the 1840s—and, as we have seen, what French Liberal intellectuals were doing from the 1810s. It is an attack on the main stock of French intellectual tradition: Guizot and Comte are as much its necessary victims as Marx.

However, there are nonintellectual reasons why, from the 1970s, such a demotion of the French Revolution became less unthinkable than it would have been before. The first is specifically French. The profound transformation of that country since the Second World War has made it, in some respects, almost unrecognisable to those who knew it before the Second World War. Much of the scepticism about whether the French Revolution was a bourgeois revolution springs from the comparison between the modernised, industrial, high-tech, urbanised France of today and the strikingly rural and petty-bourgeois France of the nineteenth century; between the France of the 1940s with its forty percent agricultural population and the France of the 1980s in which ninety percent of the population is not occupied in farming. The economic transformation of the country since the Second World War plainly has nothing to do with 1789. Then what, the observer may well reflect, did the bourgeois revolution do for capitalist development? The question is not unreasonable, although it is easy to overlook the fact that by nineteenth-century standards France was among the most developed and industrialised economies, and that the contrast between other European industrial capitalist economies before 1914 and since 1870 is probably just as striking.

Again, the view that the Revolution is no longer relevant to France, which was put forward by Furet and others during the bicentenary period, that it is finished, its work finally concluded, is at least comprehensible if we appreciate the extraordinary discontinuity between the politics of the country

DOUGLAS COLLEGE LIBRARIES

before and after the Fourth Republic—that is, the extraordinary continuity from 1789 until, say, 1958. It is indeed the case that during the whole of that period the line between political Right and Left separated those who accepted 1789 and those who refused to, and that, after the disappearance of the "Bonapartist" option (which was, in French terms, a subvariety of the revolutionary tradition), it separated those who believed in the Republic from those who rejected it. Here the Second World War marks the transformation. Unlike Pétain, whose regime had the classic marks of the anti-1789 reaction, De Gaulle, although of traditional Catholic-monarchist background, was the first genuinely Republican leader from the Right. The politics of the Fifth Republic really have been very different from those of its predecessors, although even the Fourth, with its temporary elimination of the old ultraright and the (also temporary) prominence of a Catholic-Democratic party were some way from tradition. True, the traditional Republican Left also emerged, apparently more powerful than ever, from the wartime Resistance which became the ideological legitimation of postwar France, at any rate for a generation or so. And the Republican Left, in the Radical, Socialist, or Communist version, fused the tradition of 1789 with that of the Resistance. However, that Left, in its organised form, was soon seen to be either declining or isolated. Radical Socialism, central to the Third Republic, faded away, and not even the talents of Pierre Mendès-France could arrest its decline. The Socialist party barely survived the Fourth Republic, and looked as if it would disappear from sight, until François Mitterrand recreated it in the early 1970s in a form that had little in common with the old "French Section of the Socialist International." The Communist party maintained itself for a generation within a sort of ghetto or fortress, whose defences kept the intrusions of the late twentieth century at bay, but its own decline in the 1980s was all the more spectacular. Small wonder that young or even middle-aged whiz kids from the (postwar) Ecole Nationale d'Administration or other political technocrats and commentators saw the French Revolution as something remote from current French politics.

Yet, until the 1940s, this had not been so. Even in personal terms, the Revolution was, as it were, within reach of young men and women who (like the present author) sang versions of the revolutionary *Carmagnole* directed against suitable reactionaries at demonstrations of the Popular Front in the 1930s. A mere three steps linked young revolutionaries of those years to Gracchus Babeuf, the memory of whose Conspiracy of the Equals had been perpetuated by his comrade Filippo Buonarroti (1761–1835) in an influential History.[27] Buonarroti, who has been plausibly described as "the first professional revolutionist," pioneered those secret revolutionary vanguards of which his follower Auguste Blanqui (1805–1881) became the leader and inspiration, transforming the Jacobin people into the nineteenth-century "proletariat."[28] The Paris Commune of 1871 was the brief moment of triumph for these pre-Marxian French Communists. Its last surviving member, Zéphyrin Camélinat (born 1840), had died, a member of the French Communist party, as recently as 1932.

What is more, the academic historiography of the French Revolution was itself flesh of the flesh, bone of the bone of that Third Republic whose political permanence was assured by the partnership of the descendants of 1789 liberalism and 1793 Jacobinism against the enemies of the Revolution and the Republic. This was so even biographically. Its great historians were men of the people, from families of peasants, artisans, or workers or—more likely than not—sons or wards of those primary schoolteachers who were the secular priesthood of the Republic (Soboul, Vovelle); men who reached the academic heights through the narrow, but nevertheless accessible opening that the Republican educational system gave to talent, and who themselves expected to work for their academic honours while remaining high school teachers for a large part of their careers. They were Frenchmen of the era when the *de facto* theoretical organ of the Republic, the satirical *Le Canard Enchaîné* thought of its readers as essentially men (certainly not yet women) employed by the Postal and Telegraph Services in cities like Limoges, with a hatred for priesthood and, "big money," a taste for Vouvray and Juliénas at corner cafés, a reluctance to pay taxes which were by definition excessive, and a cynical view of Radical-Socialist senators. How remote that France seems today, when even men passionately devoted to the revolutionary tradition sentimentalise it ironically as Régis Debray does, as "the garden of France as it was in 1930, that cosy hexagon of hill and grove, of local councillors and three-hundred varieties of cheese, to which Radicalism attached its Phrygian bonnet, and Jean Giraudoux his metaphors".[29]

These historians belonged to the unreconstructed, ancient, pretechnological France, even in the sense that the great Mathiez kept in touch with the world without a telephone, and neither he nor Georges Lefebvre owned a typewriter or could type.[30] They were not rich or fashionable, they were rooted in provincial towns, and if they came to Marx it was by the untheoretical high road of the French "man of the people" seeking the most radical position on the political spectrum.

Theirs was simply not the France of today, where the junior executive (*jeune cadre*) and the media-intellectual are far more central figures than the schoolmaster, and where even the institutions that provided the main form of higher education for brilliant young men from modest backgrounds, the (non-Parisian) Ecoles Normales Supérieures or senior teachers training colleges, are increasingly taken over by the children of the established upper middle class.[31]

Under the circumstances it is not surprising that the Revolution today seems considerably more remote from the realities of France than it seemed even in the 1930s, let alone in the early 1900s, the aftermath of the Dreyfus affair, when France had still appeared to be convulsed by the struggle of those who hailed the destroyers of the Bastille and those who execrated them. Paris itself, the city of the Revolution par excellence, is today a gentrified habitat of the middle classes, to which those who would once have been called "the people" commute for daily employment from outer suburbs and satellite towns, leaving most of the evening streets empty and the corner bistrots locked. Its mayor in 1989 was a Conservative ex-prime minister and the leader of the French Right, and his party controlled not only the city hall, but, without exception, every one of the capital's twenty *arrondissements*. If France has changed so drastically, why not the history of the Revolution?

Historical revisionism outside France was far less politicised, at all events since the days of Cobban, whose own revulsion against Georges Lefebvre can only be understood in the context of the liberal fears of Soviet communism and Soviet expansion in the years of the first Cold War. Cobban himself was enough of a cold warrior to help to blacklist his own pupil, the Communist schoolmaster George Rudé, whose academic career had consequently to be made not in Great Britain, but in South Australia and, later, Canada. Most revisionist researchers since then have not been moved by such obvious passions. How, then, can we explain the general scholarly retreat from the traditional interpretation during the past quarter of a century?

One reason is, of course, that historians have been increasingly moved by incentives that became more compelling as the academic profession itself expanded: by what Crane Brinton in his review of Cobban called "the compulsion—no weaker term will do—on the historian, and in particular on the young scholar seeking to establish himself, to be original.... The creative historian, like the creative artist, has in our time to produce something new as an 'interpretation.' He has, in short, to be a *revisionist*."[32] The French Revolution is by no means the only field in history where the incentive to produce a revisionist version, that is, to reject the established view, is irresistible. It is particularly visible in this field because the Revolution itself is so central a feature of our historical landscape, and because—for that very reason—its study in British and American universities has been more cultivated than most other parts of the history of foreign states. Yet, although this accounts for some of the revisionism in the field, it cannot account for all of it.

Anticommunist liberalism also obviously remains a factor of importance, and has been so ever since the late J.L. Talmon began to explore this line of thought—admittedly using a somewhat different mode of discourse—in his *Origins of Totalitarian Democracy* in the late 1940s.[33] It would be quite wrong to underestimate the sense, among some liberal historians, that Jacobinism must be rejected because of the ideological offspring it produced, although it is easier to understand such sentiments in the 1980s when they come from intellectuals in communist countries. Wajda's 1982 film *Danton* is patently not so much about Paris in the Year II as about Warsaw in 1980. Nevertheless, this is a minor factor.

On the other hand, the factors already noted in the French case also help to explain the rise of revisionism elsewhere, even if it has generated far less political, ideological, and personal ill will outside Paris. In some respects the context of non-French revisionism is more illuminating, for it allows us to see that more is involved in it than the international retreat of Marxism. That of course, is certainly involved. Marxism, as we have seen, had integrated both the early French liberal tradition and twentieth-century, leftwing Republican historiography into its own historical model of historical change through revolution. At the end of World War II a monolithic, monocentric version of Marxism, embodied in the ideology of Moscow-aligned Communist parties, was at its apogee, and the parties themselves, after the most successful period in their history, were at the peak of their size, power, and influence—not least over the left wing of Europe's intellectuals. For practical purposes, "Marxism" meant this set of doctrines, since other organisations claiming to represent this theory were—with the rarest exceptions—politically negligible, and unorthodox theorists outside or inside the Communist parties were usually isolated and marginal even within the extreme Left.[34] The national and international antifascist unity which had made this possible began to break up visibly in 1946–1948 but, paradoxically, the first Cold War helped to hold the Communist (that is, de facto the Marxist) camp together, until cracks appeared within Moscow itself in 1956.

The crises within Eastern Europe in 1956 led to a fairly massive exodus of intellectuals from the western Communist parties, although not necessarily from the Left, or even the Marxist-oriented Left. During the next decade and a half, Marxism became politically pluralist, split between Communist parties of different persuasions and international allegiances, dissident Marxist groups of various opinions which now acquired some political significance (for example, the rival sects of Trotskyism), new revolutionary groupings attracted to what was now the ideology of revolt and social revolution par excellence, and other movements or currents of the extreme Left without clear organisational or any other profiles, where Marx competed for influence with what he himself would have recognised as the heirs of Bakunin. The orthodox old Communist parties, more or less aligned with Moscow, probably remained by far the largest component of the Marxist Left in the nonsocialist world, but even within them Marxism ceased to aspire to monolithic unity, and a variety of Marxist interpretations, often associated with famous but hitherto marginalised Marxist writers from the past, or seeking to marry Marx to various important or fashionable academic doctrines, were now accepted.

The extraordinary expansion of higher education created a body of students and intellectuals enormously larger, both relatively and absolutely, than any comparable stratum had been hitherto, and this gave the political radicalisation of the 1960s, of which they became the shock troops, an unusual taste for theoretical reading and discussion, or at any rate for the use of a jargon based on phrases taken from academic theorists. Paradoxically, the peak of this new, if confused, flowering of Marxist writing and reading coincided with the peak of the wave of global prosperity—the boom years immediately before the oil crisis of 1973. In the 1970s and 1980s the Marxist Left was in retreat both politically and ideologically. By this time the crisis affected not only nongovernmental Marxism, but also the hitherto rigid and officially obligatory doctrines of countries under communist regimes (which, however, no longer shared a single dogmatic version of their state religion). The French Revolution, as part of the Marxist pedigree, was an obvious victim of this process.

Yet, in a more general sense, the profound social, economic, and cultural transformation of the globe since 1950—and especially of the advanced countries of capitalism—could not but lead to a rethinking within the Marxist Left, or rather within the increasingly subdivided and impermanent Marxist Lefts. Thus, the changes in the position of the industrial proletariat, which, even if it had shown signs of wanting to be, no longer looked large enough to be a very plausible gravedigger of capitalism, and the changes in the structures and prospects of capitalism were bound to gnaw away some of the edges of the traditional theories of both bourgeois and proletarian revolution, of which the canonical interpretation of the French Revolution had become an integral part. Indeed, the question what exactly constituted a bourgeois revolution, and whether such revolutions actually brought a bourgeoisie to power even when they occurred, began to preoccupy some Marxists (in Britain for example) in the 1960s, and a distinct retreat from the classical position could be noted.[35]

But not only Marxists. The issue of the bourgeois revolution became central to a number of debates among historians who were not in the least Marxist in orientation (except insofar as a good deal of the Marxian problematic and analysis has, over the past fifty years, been insensibly absorbed by most serious historians), and to the debates on the roots of German National Socialism in the 1960s and 1970s. If there was a

German Sonderweg that led toward Hitler, it was due to the failure of the German bourgeois revolution of 1848, unlike British and French bourgeois liberalism, which had the selfconfidence of a victorious revolution—bourgeois or otherwise—behind it. Conversely, critics of the Sonderweg thesis argued that the German bourgeoisie got the bourgeois society it wanted or needed even though it had not made a successful revolution.[36] However, revolution or no revolution, had the bourgeoisie achieved its aims anywhere? Did not, as one (leftwing) historian has argued, the old regime survive almost everywhere in Europe at the end of the nineteenth century?[37] Surely, it was convincingly maintained, even in the first industrial economy the industrialists were neither the ruling class nor by any means the richest and most influential members of the middle class.[38] What, in fact, *was* the nineteenth-century bourgeoisie? Social history, which had concentrated on investigating the working classes for a generation, now discovered that it knew very little indeed about the middle classes, and set about remedying this ignorance.[39]

Indeed, the question was far from purely academic. Thus, in the Britain of Margaret Thatcher, champions of that regime's radical neo-liberalism explained that the decline of the British economy had been due to the failure of British capitalism in the past to break decisively with the noncapitalist and aristocratic past, and thus to abandon values that stood in the way of market-led growth: in fact, that Thatcher completed the bourgeois revolution which Cromwell had left unfinished.[40] (Paradoxically this line of argument converged with one which one trend among British Marxists had used for their own purposes.)

In short, revisionism about the history of the French Revolution is merely one aspect of a much wider revisionism about the process of western—and later global—development into, and in, the era of capitalism. It does not only affect the Marxist interpretation, but most other historical interpretations of these processes, for, in light of the quite extraordinary changes that have transformed the world since the end of World War II, all of them appear to stand in need of rethinking. There is no historical precedent for changes so rapid, profound, and—in socioeconomic terms—revolutionary in so brief a period. Much that was previously unnoticed became visible in the light of this contemporary experience. Much that was taken for granted appears open to question. Moreover, it is not only the historical origins and development of modern society that ask for some reconsideration, but the very objectives of such societies, as accepted since the eighteenth century by all modern and modernising regimes, capitalist and (since 1917) socialist—notably the objective of unlimited technological progress and economic growth. The debates about what has been traditionally (and legitimately) seen as a central episode in the development of the modern world, and one of its most prominent landmarks, must be set in the wider context of a late twentieth century reconsidering its past and possible future in the light of the world transformation. But why should the French Revolution be retrospectively made into the scapegoat for our inability to understand the present?

Yet, revisionism or not, let us not forget what was obvious to all educated persons in the nineteenth century, and is still obvious: the Revolution's centrality and relevance. The very fact that after two hundred years it was the focus of passionate ideological and political debate, both academic and public, proves the point. One does not lose one's temper about dead issues. On its second centenary the French Revolution had not declined into a sort of national "Happy Birthday to You" celebration, as had the United States Bicentennial, nor into a mere excuse for tourism. Moreover, the bicentenary was more than a purely French occasion. Over a large part of the world the media of public communication, from press to television, gave it a degree of prominence hardly ever given to events in a single foreign country, and over an even larger part of the world the academics gave it their five-star treatment. Both evidently commemorated the Revolution in the belief that it was relevant to contemporary concerns.

For the French Revolution was indeed a set of events sufficiently powerful and sufficiently universal in its impact, to have transformed the world *permanently* in important respects; and to introduce, or at least to give names to, forces that continue to transform it.

Even if we leave aside France, whose legal, administrative, and educational structures are still substantially the structures given to the country by the Revolution, which established and named the departments in which Frenchmen still live, the permanent changes that can be traced back to the Revolution are substantial. Half the world's legal systems are based on the legal codification it pioneered. Countries as remote from 1789 as Islamic fundamentalist Iran are basically national territorial states structured on the model carried into the world by the Revolution, together with so much of our modern political vocabulary.[41] Every scientist in the world, and outside the United States every reader of this book, even today pays a daily tribute to the Revolution by using the metric system it invented and propagated. More concretely, the French Revolution became part of the *national* histories of large areas of Europe, America, and even the Middle East, through its direct impact on their territories and regimes—not to mention the political and ideological models derived from it, and the inspiration or fear of its example. Who could make sense of, say, German history since 1789 without it? Who, indeed, could understand anything about the history of the nineteenth century without it?

Moreover, if some of the models set up by, or in the light of, the French Revolution, are no longer of much practical interest, for example, the bourgeois revolution—although it would be unwise to say the same of others, such as the territorial citizen-state or "nation-state"—others among its innovations retain their political potential. The French Revolution gave peoples the sense that history could be changed by their action, and it gave them, incidentally, what remains to this day the single most powerful slogan ever formulated for the politics of democracy and common people which it inaugurated: Liberty, Equality, Fraternity. Nor is this historical effect of the Revolution negated by the demonstration that (except momentarily) probably most Frenchmen and an even larger majority of Frenchwomen were uninvolved in the Revolution, or inactive, or even, at times, hostile; or that, at any rate, not many of them were enthusiastic Jacobins; or that the French Revolution saw much government "on behalf of the people" and very little government *of*, let alone *by* the people, as is also the case in most other regimes since 1789; or that its leaders tended to identify "the people" with the "right-thinking" people, as is also the case in some. The French Revolution demonstrated the power of the common people in a manner that no subsequent government has ever allowed itself to forget—if only in the form of untrained, improvised, conscript armies, defeating the conjunction of the finest and most experienced troops of the old regimes.

In fact, the paradox of revisionism is that it seeks to diminish the historic significance and transforming capacity of a revolution whose extraordinary and lasting impact are utterly obvious, or that can be overlooked only by a combination of intellectual provincialism and tunnel vision;[42] or by the monographic myopia which is the occupational disease of specialist research in historical archives.

The power of the people, which is not the same as the domesticated version of it that is expressed in periodic elections by universal suffrage, is rarely seen, and even more rarely exercised. Yet, when it is seen, as it was on several continents and occasions in the bicentenary year of the French Revolution—when it transformed the countries of Eastern Europe —it is an overwhelmingly impressive spectacle. In no revolution before 1789 was it more evident, more immediately effective, and more decisive. It was what turned the French Revolution into a revolution. For there can be no revisionism about the fact that "up to the early summer of 1789, the conflict between 'aristocrats' and 'patriots' in the National Assembly had resembled the kinds of struggles over a constitution which had racked most western European countries from the mid-century on.... When the common people did intervene in July and August 1789, they transformed conflict among elites into something quite different," if only by bringing about, within a matter of weeks, the collapse of state power and administration and the power of the rural ruling class in the countryside.[43] This is what gave the *Declaration of the Rights of Man* a far greater international resonance than the American models that inspired it; what made the innovations of France—including its new political vocabulary—more readily accepted outside; which created its ambiguities and conflicts; and, not least, what turned it into the epic, the terrible, the spectacular, the apocalyptic event which gave it a sort of uniqueness, both horrifying and inspiring.

This is what made men and women think of it as "the most terrible and momentous series of events in all history."[44] This is what made Thomas Carlyle write: "To me it often seems, as if the right *History* (that impossible thing I mean by History) of the French Revolution were the grand Poem of our Time, as if the man who *could* write the *truth* of that, were worth all other writers and singers."[45] And it is this that made it senseless for the historian to pick and choose the parts of that great upheaval that deserve commendation and those that should be rejected. The Revolution that became "the real starting-point in the history of the nineteenth century" is not this or that episode between 1789 and 1815, but the whole of it.[46]

Fortunately, it is still alive. For Liberty, Equality, Fraternity and the values of reason and the Enlightenment—the values on which modern civilisation has been built, from the days of the American Revolution—are more needed than ever, as irrationalism, fundamentalist religion, obscurantism, and barbarity are once again gaining on us. So it is a good thing that in the year of the bicentenary we had occasion to think again about the extraordinary historical events that transformed the world two centuries ago. For the better.

Appendix

The following passages from the notebooks of Antonio Gramsci, former leader of the Italian Communist Party, written in a fascist jail at various times from 1929 to 1934, indicate how a highly intelligent Marxist revolutionary used what he took to be the experience and significance of the Jacobinism of 1793–1794, both for purposes of historical understanding and for contemporary political analysis. The starting point is a series of reflections on the Italian Risorgimento, whose most radical group, Mazzini's Action Party, is compared unfavourably with the Jacobins. Apart from some interesting observations on why the "bourgeoisie" is not necessarily the political ruling class in "bourgeois regimes," Gramsci's notes essentially turn on the (unspoken) comparison of two historic "vanguards": the Jacobins within the framework of bourgeois revolution and the Bolsheviks, at least in his concept of their Italian version, in the era of the socialist revolution. It will be evident that Gramsci saw the task of the revolutionaries not only in class terms, but (perhaps primarily) in terms of the nation led by a class.

For the source of his interpretation of Jacobinism—essentially the postwar writings of Mathiez, whom he read in prison—and for a fuller critical commentary, see Renato Zangheri, "Gramsci e il giacobinismo" Passato e Presente 19: Rivista di storia contemporanea (Jan–April 1989): 155–164. The present text is taken from Quintin Hoare and Geoffrey Nowell Smith eds., Antonio Gramsci, Selections from

115

the Prison Notebooks *(London: Lawrence and Wishart, 1971), pp. 77–83.*

* * *

On the subject of Jacobinism and the Action Party, an element to be highlighted is the following: that the Jacobins won their function of "leading" [*dirigente*] party by a struggle to the death; they literally "imposed" themselves on the French bourgeoisie, leading it into a far more advanced position than the originally strongest bourgeois nuclei would have spontaneously wished to take up, and even far more advanced than that which the historical premises should have permitted—hence the various forms of backlash and the function of Napoleon I. This feature, characteristic of Jacobinism (but before that, also of Cromwell and the "Roundheads") and hence of the entire French Revolution, which consists in (apparently) forcing the situation, in creating irreversible *faits accomplis*, and in a group of extremely energetic and determined men driving the bourgeois forward with kicks in the backside, may be schematised in the following way. The Third Estate was the least homogeneous; it had a very disparate intellectual élite, and a group which was very advanced economically but politically moderate. Events developed along highly interesting lines. The representatives of the Third Estate initially only posed those questions which interested the actual physical members of the social group, their immediate "corporate" interests (corporate in the traditional sense, of the immediate and narrowly selfish interests of a particular category). The precursors of the Revolution were in fact moderate reformers, who shouted very loud but actually demanded very little. Gradually a new élite was selected out which did not concern itself solely with "corporate" reforms, but tended to conceive of the bourgeoisie as the hegemonic group of all the popular forces. This selection occurred through the action of two factors: the resistance of the old social forces, and the international threat. The old forces did not wish to concede anything, and if they did concede anything they did it with the intention of gaining time and preparing a counter-offensive. The Third Estate would have fallen into these successive "pitfalls" without the energetic action of the Jacobins, who opposed every "intermediate" halt in the revolutionary process, and sent to the guillotine not only the elements of the old society which was hard a-dying, but also the revolutionaries of yesterday—today become reactionaries. The Jacobins, consequently, were the only party of the revolution in progress, in as much as they not only represented the immediate needs and aspirations of the actual physical individuals who constituted the French bourgeoisie, but they also represented the revolutionary movement as a whole, as an integral historical development. For they represented future needs as well, and, once again, not only the needs of those particular physical individuals, but also of all the national groups which had to be assimilated to the existing fundamental group. It is necessary to insist against a tendentious and fundamentally anti-historical school of thought, that the Jacobins were realists of the Machiavelli stamp and not abstract dreamers. They were convinced of the absolute truth of their slogans about equality, fraternity and liberty, and, what is more important, the great popular masses whom the Jacobins stirred up and drew into the struggle were also convinced of their truth. The Jacobins' language, their ideology, their methods of action reflected perfectly the exigencies of the epoch, even if "today", in a different situation and after more than a century of cultural evolution, they may appear "abstract" and "frenetic". Naturally they reflected those exigencies according to the French cultural tradition. One proof of this is the analysis of Jacobin language which is to be found in *The Holy Family*. Another is Hegel's admission, when he places as parallel and reciprocally translatable the juridico-political language of the Jacobins and the concepts of classical German philosophy—which is recognised today to have the maximum of concreteness and which was the source of modern historicism. The first necessity was to annihilate the enemy forces, or at least to reduce them to impotence in order to make a counter-revolution impossible. The second was to enlarge the cadres of the bourgeoisie as such, and to place the latter at the head of all the national forces; this meant identifying the interests and the requirements common to all the national forces, in order to set these forces in motion and lead them into the struggle, obtaining two results: (*a*) that of opposing a wider target to the blows of the enemy, i.e. of creating a politico-military relation favourable to the revolution; (*b*) that of depriving the enemy of every zone of passivity in which it would be possible to enrol Vendée-type armies. Without the agrarian policy of the Jacobins, Paris would have had the Vendée at its very doors. The resistance of the Vendée properly speaking is linked to the national question, which had become envenomed among the peoples of Brittany and in general among those alien to the slogan of the "single and indivisible republic" and to the policy of bureaucratic-military centralisation—a slogan and a policy which the Jacobins could not renounce without committing suicide. The Girondins tried to exploit federalism in order to crush Jacobin Paris, but the provincial troops brought to Paris went over to the revolutionaries. Except for certain marginal areas, where the national (and linguistic) differentiation was very great, the agrarian question proved stronger than aspirations to local autonomy. Rural France accepted the hegemony of Paris; in other words, it understood that in order definitively to destroy the old régime it had to make a bloc with the most advanced elements of the Third Estate, and not with the Girondin moderates. If it is true that the Jacobins "forced" its hand, it is also true that this always occurred in the direction of real historical development. For not only did they organise a bourgeois government, i.e. make the bourgeoisie the dominant class—they did more. They created the bourgeois State, made the bourgeoisie into the leading, hegemonic class of the nation, in other words gave the new State a permanent basis and created the compact modern French nation.

That the Jacobins, despite everything, always remained on bourgeois ground is demonstrated by the events which marked their end, as a party cast in too specific and inflexible a mould, and by the death of Robespierre. Maintaining the Le Chapelier law, they were not willing to concede to the workers the right of combination; as a consequence they had to pass the law of the *maximum*. They thus broke the Paris urban bloc: their assault forces, assembled in the Commune, dispersed in disappointment, and Thermidor gained the upper hand. The Revolution had found its widest class limits. The policy of alliances and of permanent revolution had finished by posing new questions which at that time could not be resolved; it had unleashed elemental forces which only a military dictatorship was to succeed in containing.

If in Italy a Jacobin party was not formed, the reasons are to be sought in the economic field, that is to say in the relative weakness of the Italian bourgeoisie and in the different historical climate in Europe after 1815. The limit reached by the Jacobins, in their policy of forced reawakening of French popular energies to be allied with the bourgeoisie, with the Le Chapelier law and that of the *maximum*, appeared in 1848 as a "spectre" which was already threatening—and this was skilfully exploited by Austria, by the old governments and even by Cavour (quite apart from the Pope). The bourgeoisie could not (perhaps) extend its hegemony further over the great popular strata—which it did succeed in embracing in France—(could not for subjective rather than objective reasons); but action directed at the peasantry was certainly always possible. Differences between France, Germany and Italy in the process by which the bourgeoisie took power (and England). It was in France that the process was richest in developments, and in active and positive political elements. In Germany, it evolved in ways which in certain aspects resembled what happened in Italy, and in others what happened in England. In Germany, the movement of 1848 failed as a result of the scanty bourgeois concentration (the Jacobin-type slogan was furnished by the democratic Far Left: "permanent revolution"), and because the question of renewal of the State was intertwined with the national question. The wars of 1864, 1866 and 1870 resolved both the national question and, in an intermediate form, the class question: the bourgeoisie obtained economic-industrial power, but the old feudal classes remained as the government stratum of the political State, with wide corporate privileges in the army, the administration and on the land. Yet at least, if these old classes kept so much importance in Germany and enjoyed so many privileges, they exercised a national function, became the "intellectuals" of the bourgeoisie, with a particular temperament conferred by their caste origin and by tradition. In England, where the bourgeois revolution took place before that in France, we have a similar phenomenon to the German one of fusion between the old and the new—this notwithstanding the extreme energy of the English "Jacobins", i.e. Cromwell's "roundheads". The old aristocracy remained as a governing stratum, with certain privileges, and it too became the intellectual stratum of the English bourgeoisie (it should be added that the English aristocracy has an open structure, and continually renews itself with elements coming from the intellectuals and the bourgeoisie). In Germany, despite the great capitalist development, the class relations created by industrial development, with the limits of bourgeois hegemony reached and the position of the progressive classes reversed, have induced the bourgeoisie not to struggle with all its strength against the old régime, but to allow a part of the latter's façade to subsist, behind which it can disguise its own real domination.

Notes

Preface

1. Reported in *Le Monde* 11 January 1988.
2. Jonathan Clark in *Sunday Times* Book supplement 21 May 1989, p. 69.
3. Since the present author, sceptical of political revisionism, has been very closely associated with this journal, I cannot be accused of lacking interest in new departures in historical research on the Revolution.
4. See E.J. Hobsbawm, "The Making of a Bourgeois Revolution" *Social Research* 56, no. 1 (1989): 10–11.
5. "schon mit einer gewissen Selbstverständlichkeit gebraucht" Ernst Nolte, *Marxismus und Industrielle Revolution* (Stuttgart, 1983), p. 24.

Chapter 1: A Revolution of the Middle Class

1. J. Holland Rose. *A Century of Continental History. 1780–1880* (London, 1895), p. 1.
2. *Allgemeine Geschichte vom Anfang der historischen Kenntnisz bis auf unsere Zeiten*, vol. 9 (Braunschweig, 1848), pp. 1–2.
3. Ibid.
4. See Barton R. Friedman's *Fabricating History: English Writers on the French Revolution* (Princeton, 1988), p. 117.
5. François Furet and Denis Richet, *La Révolution française* (Paris, 1970).

6. Eberhard Schmitt and Matthias Meyn, "Ursprung und Charakter der Französischen Revolution bei Marx und Engels," in Ernst Hinrichs, Eberhard Schmitt, and Rudolf Vierhaus, eds., *Vom Ancien Regime zur Französischen Revolution* (Göttingen, Vandenhoeck, and Rupprecht, 1978), pp. 588–649.

7. *Past & Present* 60 (1973): 469–96; and in Douglas Johnson, ed., *French Society and the Revolution* (Cambridge, 1976), p. 90.

8. Marx to Weydemeyer, 5 March 1852, Marx to Engels, 27 July 1854, from Karl Marx and Frederick Engels, *Collected Works*, vol. 39 (London, 1983), pp. 62–63, 473–76.

9. For his (posthumously published) "L'Esprit de la Révolution," see *Oeuvres du comte P.L. Roederer publiées par son fils A.M. Roederer* (Paris, 1854), vol. 3, pp. 7, 10–11.

10. Marcel Gauchet, "Les Lettres sur l'histoire de France de Augustin Thierry," in Pierre Nora, ed., *Les Lieux de mémoire*, vol. 2 of *La Nation* (Paris 1986), p. 271.

11. Augustin Thierry, *Essai sur l'histoire de la formation et des progrès du Tiers Etat* (Paris, 1853), p. 21.

12. Lionel Gossman, *Augustin Thierry and Liberal Historiography History and Theory* Beiheft 15 (Middletown, 1976): 37–39 for references.

13. François Guizot, *Histoire de la civilisation en Europe*, ed. Pierre Rosanvallon (Paris: Pluriel, 1985), p. 181.

14. Ibid., p. 182.

15. Ibid., pp. 181–184.

16. Ibid., p. 183.

17. W.G. Runciman, "Unnecessary Revolution: The Case of France," *Archives européennes de sociologie*, 24 (1983): 298.

18. Paul Imbs, ed., *Trésor de la langue française, Dictionnaire de la langue du xixe et du xx siècle* (Paris, 1971) vol. 5 (1977), pp. 143, 144; vol 10 (1983), p. 927.

19. It is most commonly ascribed to J.C.M. Vincent de Gournay (1712–1759).

20. *La Grande Encyclopédie* (Paris, n.d.), 30, s.v. "Smith, Adam."

21. *Catalogue général des livres imprimés de la Bibliothèque Nationale* (Paris, 1948). One might add that two English editions were also acquired during this period (1799, 1814), in addition to the first three editions already there before 1789, and the (English) abridgment of the work (1804). A French translation of Smith's *Philosophical Essays* was also published in 1797.

22. The earliest discussion in A. Bezanson, "The Early Use of the Term Industrial Revolution," *Quarterly Journal of Economics* 36 (1922): 343–349; also Ernst Nolte, *Marxismus und Industrielle Revolution* (Stuttgart, 1983), pp. 23–25.

23. Victor Cousin, *Introduction to the History of Philosophy*, trans. Henning Gottfried Linberg (Boston, 1832), p. 8.

24. *Cours de philosophie par V. Cousin: Introduction à l'histoire de la philosophie* (Paris, 1828), pp. 10–12.

25. Ibid., pp. 14–15. My translation.

26. A.F. Mignet, *Histoire de la Révolution française, depuis 1789 jusqu'en 1814*, vol. 1 (Paris, 1898), p. 15.

27. Ibid., pp. 206, 209.

28. I give the translation, presumably by the editor, in Walter Simon, ed., *French Liberalism 1789–1848* (New York, 1972), pp. 139–143.

29. Alexis de Tocqueville, *Recollections*, ed. J.P. Mayer (New York, 1949), p. 2.

30. Ibid.

31. De Tocqueville's *Ancien Régime*, trans. M.W. Paterson (Oxford, 1947), p. 23.

32. Runciman, "Unnecessary Revolution," p. 318; Jacques Solé, *La révolution en questions* (Paris, 1988), pp. 273, 275.

33. Lorenz Stein, *Der Socialismus und Communismus des heutigen Frankreich: Ein Beitrag zur Zeitgeschichte*, 2d ed. (Leipzig, 1848), pp. 128–129, 131.

34. Ibid.

35. Guizot, *Histoire de la civilisation*, pp. 181–182.

36. A full discussion in Jürgen Kocka and Ute Frevert, eds., *Bürgertum im 19 Jahrhundert*, 3 vols. (Munich, 1988), esp. vol. 1, part 1.

37. Gossman, *Thierry*, p. 40.

38. Thierry, *Tiers Etat*, pp. 76–77.

39. Guizot, *Histoire de la civilisation*, pp. 182–183.

40. Ibid., pp. 287–288.

41. Cf. Guizot in Simon, ed., *French Liberalism*, p. 108. The influence both of Thierry's equation of race and class struggles and of Walter Scott's *Ivanhoe* is evident here.

42. Lord Acton, *Lectures on the French Revolution* (London, 1910), p. 2. The lectures, published posthumously, were originally given in 1895.

43. Wilhelm Friedrich Volger, *Handbuch der allgemeinen Weltgeschichte*, vol. 2, pt. 2: *Neueste Geschichte* (Hanover, 1839), p. 240.

44. *Geschichtliche Grundbegriffe*, ed. O. Brunner, W. Conze, and R. Koselleck (Stuttgart, 1972), s.v. "Bürger," pp. 715–716.

45. Ibid., vol. 5, p. 747, s.v. "Revolution." Even toward the end of the century the same theme still occurs in the *Brockhaus Conversationslexikon*, 13th ed. (Leipzig, 1886), vol. 13, p. 652, article "Revolution." The English and French revolutions are bracketed as the "two catastrophes which mark a veritable turning-point in the cultural life of Europe, and to which the other violent changes of the epoch are more or less linked."

46. In his *Politique libérale ou défense de la Révolution française* (1860) cited in Alice Gérard, *La Révolution française: Mythes et interprétations 1789–1970* (Paris, 1970), p. 37.

47. Ibid., p. 34.

48. In "Chartism," *Critical and Miscellaneous Essays* (London, 1899), vol. 4, p. 149. Carlyle argues that the French Revolution is not yet complete: "It was a revolt of the oppressed lower classes against the oppressing or neglecting upper classes: not a French revolt only; no, a European one."

49. Notably in the extraordinary docudrama *Danton's Tod*.

50. Friedrich List, *Schriften, Reden, Briefe* (Berlin, 1932) vol. 1, p. 286. The passage is undated, but written between 1815 and 1825.

51. Carl Richter, *Staats—und Gesellschaftsrecht der Französischen Revolution von 1789 bis 1804* (Berlin, 1866) vol. 1, p. viii.

52. See Constant V. Wurzbach, *Biographisches Lexikon des Kaiserthums Österreich* (Vienna, 1874), vol. 26, p. 63.

53. Cf. "La classe moyenne est arrivé au pouvoir" (Maurice de Guérin,"Correspondance 1824–1839" in *Oeuvres Complètes*, ed. B. d'Harcourt (Paris, 1947), p. 165 (citation from 1834). Edouard Alletz, *De la démocratie nouvelle ou des moeurs et de la puissance des classes moyennes en France* (Paris, 1837) 2 vols: Jules Michelet: "La classe moyenne bourgeoise, dont la partie la plus inquiète s'agitait aux Jacobins" *Histoire de la Révolution Française* cited in *Dictionnaire Robert* (Paris, 1978), vol. 4, p. 533.

54. Thierry, *Réorganisation de la société européenne* (1814), cited in Gossman, *Thierry*, p. 37.

55. Cited in Simon, *French Liberalism*, p. 142.

56. For a convenient conspectus of the evolution of the word as a political term, see the article "Liberalismus" by Ulrich Dierse in *Historisches Wörterbuch der Philosophie*, ed. Joachim Ritter and Karlfried Gründer (Basel-Stuttgart, 1980), vol. 5, cols. 257–271, which argues that its use—by future Liberals like Sieyès and Constant—was not yet sufficiently specific before 1814. The first political group under that label is found in Spain, 1810, where deputies were grouped into "liberales" and "serviles", and the Spanish terminology was undoubtedly influential in securing the fortunes of the term.

57. Albert Venn Dicey, "Taine's Origins of Contemporary France," *The Nation* 12 April, 1894, pp. 274–276.

58. Runciman, "Unnecessary Revolution," p. 315; cf. François Furet, *Interpreting the French Revolution* (Cambridge, 1981), p. 119.

59. De Tocqueville, *Ancien Régime*, p. 176.

60. Cited in Gossman, *Thierry*, p. 39.

61. Cited in Simon, *French Liberalism*, pp. 149–141.

62. René Sédillot, *Le coût de la Révolution française* (Paris, 1987), pp. 282–277.

63. But, of course, although sceptics see a "bilan globalement négatif" in agriculture, as elsewhere; even Sédillot does not actually deny that "the peasants gained more than they lost" (Ibid, p. 173, 266), which is what everyone in the nineteenth century took for granted.

64. *Essays on the Early Period of the French Revolution by the Late John Wilson Croker* (London, 1857), p. 2.

65. Ibid.

66. *Nouvelle Biographie Générale* (Paris, 1855), vol. 13, p. 810. Nineteenth-century readers did not need to be told that Phaeton was an early astronaut of Greek myth who was incinerated when his chariot came too close to the sun.

67. In the (uncompleted) second part of his *Ancien Régime*. See Alan Kahan. "Tocqueville's Two Revolutions," *Journal of the History of Ideas* 46 (1985): 595–596.

68. Cited in Stanley Mellon, *The Political Uses of History: A Study of Historians in the French Restoration* (Stanford, 1958), p. 29.

69. Ibid.

70. Gossman, *Thierry*, p. 7.

71. See Mellon, *Political Uses of History*, pp. 47–52, for this line of argument.

72. Stein, *Der Socialismus*, p. 133.

73. Cited in Simon, *French Liberalism*, p. 110.

74. Ibid., pp. 112, 113.

75. Cited from "Bezwaaren tegen den geest der eeuw" (1823) in the entry "Liberalisme" (*Woordenboek der Nederlandsche Taal* vol. 8, part i (The Hague, 1916), p. 1874.

76. Mignet, *Histoire*, p. 207.

Chapter 2: Beyond the Bourgeoisie

1. Maurice Agulhon, *La République au village: Les populations du Var de la Révolution à la Seconde République* (Paris, 1970).

2. Cf. Hans-Ulrich Wehler, *Deutsche Gesellschaftsgeschichte Zweiter Band 1815–1849* (Munich, 1987), pp. 706–715, and the large bibliography in ibid, pp. 880–882.

3. See his pamphlet, addressed to the rural population, *Der hessische Landbote* (1834) in Georg Büchner, *Werke und Briefe* (Munich, Deutscher Taschenbuchverlag, 1965) 133–143.

4. William Sewell, *Work and Revolution in France* (Cambridge, 1980), pp. 198–200.

5. For good examples of a "Proletarier-Marseillaise" and of the symbolic and iconographic heritage of 1789, see pp. 65, 68 of the Feltrinelli Library's *Ogni Anno un Maggio Nuovo: il Centenario del Primo Maggio*, intro. Antonio Pizzinato (Milan, 1988). This May Day centenary volume was published under the patronage of the labour unions of Umbria. See also Andrea Panaccione ed., *The Memory of May Day: An Iconographic History of the Origins and Implanting of a Workers' Holiday* (Venice: Marsilio Editore, 1989), especially p. 290 (Denmark), p. 295 (Sweden), p. 336 (Italy).

6. Lorenz Stein, *Der Socialismus*. The *von* came later when the author was a professor in Vienna.

7. Cf. "The Commune as Symbol and Example," in Georges Haupt *Aspects of International Socialism* (Cambridge and Paris, 1986), pp. 23–47.

8. "Souvenirs," in *Oeuvres Complètes* (Paris, 1964), vol. 12, p. 87.

9. Cited in Felix Gilbert's article "Revolution" in *Dictionary of the History of Ideas*, 5 vols. (New York: Scribner's Sons, 1980), p. 159.

10. Cited in Norman Stone, *Europe Transformed 1878–1919* (London, 1983), p. 331.

11. 6:118–123, July 1917, no. 1, p. 11.

12. *Geschichtliche Grundbegriffe*, vol. 5, p. 744, s.v. "Revolution".

13. Louis Blanc, *Histoire de la Révolution française* (Paris, 1847), vol. 1, p. 121.

14. Thierry, *Tiers Etat*, p. 2.

15. Marx and Engels, *Collected Works* 39, p. 474.

16. See E.J. Hobsbawm, "Marx, Engels and Politics" in E.J. Hobsbawm, ed., *The History of Marxism. Volume One: Marxism in Marx' Day* (Bloomington, 1982); *Marx en Perspective*, ed. Bernard Chavance (Paris, 1985). pp. 557–570; *"Moralising Criticism and Critical Morality"* (1847), Karl Marx and Frederick Engels, *Collected Works* (London, 1976), vol. 6, p. 319.

17. Samuel Bernstein, *Auguste Blanqui and the Art of Insurrection* (London, 1971), pp. 270–275; Engels, "The Festival of Nations in London," in *Collected Works*, vol. 6, pp. 4–5.

18. Ibid., and "The Civil War in Switzerland", *Collected Works*, vol. 6, p. 372; Marx, "Moralizing Criticism", *Collected Works*, vol. 6, p. 319.

19. Karl Marx and Frederick Engels, *Collected Works*, vol. 6 (London, 1976), p. 545.

20. See Victor Daline, "Lénine et le Jacobinisme" *Annales Historiques de la Révolution Française* 43 (1971), pp. 89–112.

21. Daniel Guérin, "Controverse sur la Révolution Française," *Cahiers Bernard Lazare*, nos. 119–120 (Paris, 1987), pp. 58–81.

22. On the prevalence of the Marseillaise in international socialist circles in the 1890s, cf. Maurice Dommanget, *Eugène Pottier: Membre de la Commune et chantre de l'Internationale* (Paris, 1971), pp. 144–146.

23. Cited in Georges Haupt, *Programm und Wirklichkeit: Die internationale sozialdemokratie vor 1914* (Neuwied, 1970), p. 141.

24. *Geschichte der Revolutionszeit von 1789 bis 1795* (1789 bis 1800) [sic]. Dritte vermehrte und verbesserte Auflage. 5 vols. (Dusseldorf, 1865–1874), vol. 1.

25. As in the entry "Bonapartismus" in Meyer's *Konversationslexikon*, 9th ed. (Mannheim, 1960), vol. 4, p. 483.

26. See Charles Rihs, *La Commune de Paris 1871: Sa structure et ses doctrines* (Paris, 1973), passim, but especially— for the imitation of the past—pp. 58–59, 182–183; for Delescluze, pp. 185–191.

27. Sanford Elwitt, *The Making of the Third Republic: Class and Politics in France, 1868–1884* (Baton Rouge, 1975), chapter 1.

28. For Garibaldi's own account, see D. Mack Smith, ed., *Garibaldi: A Portrait in Documents* (Florence, 1982), pp. 13–14.

29. Gérard, *La Révolution française*, p. 81.

30. Samuel H. Baron, *Plekhanov: the father of Russian Marxism* (London, 1963), p. 358.

31. Cf. the speech at the Petersburg Soviet on 5 November, reported in Leon Trotsky, *1905* (Harmondsworth, 1973), pp. 185 ff.

32. Daline, "Lenine et le Jacobinisme," p. 96.

33. W.H. Chamberlin, "Bolshevik Russia and Jacobin France" *The Dial.* no. 67, 12 July 1919, pp. 14–16; Charles W. Thompson "The French and Russian Revolutions" *Current History Magazine, New York Times* 13 (January, 1921), pp. 149–157.

34. Adam Ulam, *Russia's Failed Revolutions: From Decembrists to Dissidents* (London, 1981), pp. 316–317.

35. Leon Trotsky, *History of the Russian Revolution* (London, 1936), pp. 194, 589, 1204.

36. Baron, *Plekhanov*, p. 358.

37. Karl Kautsky, *Bolshevism at a Deadlock* (London, 1931), sec. IIId, "Jacobins or Bonapartists" esp. pp. 127, 135. The date of the original German edition is 1930.

38. Cited in Gérard, *La Révolution française*, p. 81.

39. *Le Bolchevisme et le Jacobinisme* (Paris, 1920), p. 24.

40. Daline, "Lenine et le Jacobinisme," p. 107.

41. "Now I find myself approving, without reservation—even with enthusiasm—the force (vigore) and harshness Stalin applied against those held to be (indicati) enemies of socialism and agents of imperialism. Faced with the capitulation of the western democracies Stalin heeded the old lesson of Jacobin terror, of implacable violence in defence of the fatherland of socialism." Giorgio Amendola, *Lettere a Milano: Ricordi e Documenti, 1939–1945* (Rome, 1973), pp. 17–18. Amendola, as the record shows, was far from

a sectarian hard-liner, or a blind loyalist. Cited in Giuseppe Boffa, *Il fenomeno Stalin nella storia del XX secolo* (Bari, 1982), p. 137.

42. Sylvain Molinier in *La Pensée* (March–April, 1947), p. 116.

43. Isaac Deutscher, *Stalin: A Political Biography*, rev. ed. (Hardmonds-worth: Penguin Books, 1966), p. 550.

44. Mahendra Nath Roy, *The Russian Revolution* (Calcutta, 1945), pp. 14–15, Trotsky, *Russian Revolution*, pp. 663–664.

45. Chamberlin, "Bolshevik Russia", pp. 14–25.

46. For references, see Boffa, *Il fenomeno Stalin*, p. 138; Stephen F. Cohen, *Bukharin and the Bolshevik Revolution* (London, 1974), pp. 131–132.

47. "Nevertheless today we must admit that the analogy of Thermidor served to becloud rather than to clarify the question," *The Workers' State and the Question of Thermidor and Bonapartism* (1935, London, 1973), p. 31.

48. Isaac Deutscher, *The Prophet Unarmed: Trotsky, 1921–1929* (Oxford, 1970).

49. Ibid., pp. 312, 313.

50. Ibid., p. 312.

51. Ibid., p. 437.

52. See Ibid., pp. 435–437.

53. Ibid., p. 437.

54. Ibid., pp. 458–459.

55. This is the version in Cohen, *Bukharin*, p. 131. Deutscher, *Prophet Unarmed*, pp. 160–163, is more nuanced.

56. Deutscher, *Prophet Unarmed*, pp. 342–345.

57. Ibid., pp. 244–245.

58. Roy, *Russian Revolution*, pp. 14–15.

59. I am inclined to follow Moshe Lewin in *Lenin's Last Struggle* (New York, 1968), who sees Lenin in his last years as backing gradual evolution. However, the question, although it has today become politically important in the USSR, is speculative. Lenin ceased effective activity in March, 1923. What he might have thought or done had he lived to judge the situation in 1927 or 1937 we can only guess.

60. Cited in Cohen, *Bukharin*, p. 133.

61. "Better Fewer but Better," *Pravda*, 2 March, 1923, printed in *Collected Works*, 4th ed. (Moscow, 1960), vol. 38, pp. 487–502.

62. The phrase was reported to me by one expert in the history of Bolshevism who had heard it in Moscow. Consultation with experts in early Soviet history from Britain, the USA and the USSR has failed to turn up any possible source for this phrase from Lenin's untranslated writings or the memoir literature about his last years.

63. Georg Forster, *Im Anblick des grossen Rades, Schriften zur Revolution*, ed. R.R. Wuthenow (Darmstadt-Neuwied, 1981), pp. 133–134.

64. (7 Nov O.S. 1917), *Collected Works*, vol. 26, pp. 291–292.

65. *Collected Works*, vol. 24, p. 267 (Speech to the 7th All-Russian Conference of the RSDLP, April 1917).

66. "Letter to American Workers," *Collected Works*, vol. 28, p. 83.

67. "Political parties in Russia and the tasks of the proletariat" (April 1917), *Collected Works*, vol. 24, p. 103.

68. "On the Revision of the Party Programme" (October, 1917), *Collected Works*, vol. 26, pp. 171–172.

69. Cited in Robert C. Tucker, *The Lenin Anthology* (New York, 1975), p. 706.

70. Ibid.

71. Evgenii Ambarzumov, "Gorbaciov, guardati dai burocrati," *Unità* (29 May 1989), p. 1. Ambarzumov was actually mistaken: in 1789 the Third Estate had two deputies for every one from each of the other two Estates, and thus formed half of the total assembly. Perhaps this is a sign that, although the memory of the French Revolution is alive in general terms, seventy years have dimmed the detailed knowledge of it in Russia that was once so striking.

Chapter 3: From One Centenary to Another

1. E.J. Hobsbawm and T. Ranger, eds., *The Invention of Tradition* (Cambridge, 1983), p. 272.

2. See M.L. Neiman, "Leninskii plan 'monumentalnoi propagandy' i pervye skulpturnye pamyatniki" (in *Istoriya Russkogo Isskusstva*, vol. 6 [Moscow, 1957], pp. 23–53), which says that Lenin got the idea from Tommaso Campanella's utopia "City of the Sun." For a brief sketch of the episode in English, see Christine Lodder, *Russian Constructivism* (New Haven, Conn.: Yale University Press, 1983), p. 53 ff. A Stigalev, "S. Konenkov i monumentalnaya propaganda" (*Sovietskaya Skulptura* no. 74 [Moscow 1976]: 210–223) provides details of how the list of sixty-six eminent subjects was drawn up, and a photo of Lenin unveiling Konenkov's Stenka Razin monument on Red Square. Between 1918 and 1920, twenty-five monuments were erected in Moscow, fifteen in Leningrad. *Sovietskoe Isskusstvo 20–30 Godakh* (Leningrad, 1988), plate 41, reproduces Lebedeva's relief of Robespierre. For other pictures of the 1918 monuments see Lodder, *Constructivism, Istoriya Russkogo Isskusstva XI, Serdzom Slushaya Revolutsiya: Isskusstvo Pervikh Let Oktyabra* (Leningrad, 1977) and *Shagi Sovietov: Kinokamera pishet istoriyu 1917–1936* (Moscow, 1979), which reproduces stills from contemporary newsreels.

3. *The Times*, (4 May 1889), p. 7a.

4. Ibid.

5. *New York Times*, (14 July 1889), p. 9.

6. Pascal Ory, "Le Centenaire de la Révolution Française," in P. Nora, ed. *Les Lieux de mémoire*, vol. 1 *La République* (Paris, 1984), pp. 523–560, for all this and more on the French aspects of the centenary.

7. Henry Dunckley, "Two Political Centenaries," *Contemporary Review* 55 (1888): 52–72.

8. "Lord Acton on the French Revolution," *The Nation* 92 (30 March 1911), pp. 318–320. Lord Acton, *Lectures on the French Revolution* (London, 1910) was published posthumously.

9. "Le banquet du centenaire de 1789," in A. Leroy-Beaulieu, *La Révolution et le Libéralisme* (Paris, 1890), pp. 1–84.

10. "The Centenary of 1789," *Edinburgh Review*, vol. 169, pp. 519–536.

11. "Taine's Conquest of the Jacobins," *Edinburgh Review* 155: 1–26.

12. Ibid.

13. B.M. Gardiner in *The Academy* 27 (4 April 1885), pp. 233–234.

14. *Edinburgh Review*, "The Centenary," pp. 521–22.

15. Ibid., pp. 534–535.

16. Goldwin Smith, "The Invitation to Celebrate the French Revolution," *National Review*, (August 1888), 729–47; "The Centenary of 1789": 522.

17. Ibid.

18. *Edinburgh Review*, A.R.D. Eliot, "The French Revolution and Modern France," *Edinburgh Review* 187: pp. 522–548.

19. *Edinburgh Review*, "The Centenary", 524.

20. Smith, "Invitation," p. 743.

21. *The Times*, (27 August 1889), 3d: "Revolution is thus far a failure. Thirteen constitutions in a century ... manifestly reflect little lustre on the men who ushered in this chronic instability."

22. Review of Alphonse Aulard's *French Revolution* in *The Spectator*, 15 October, 1910, p. 608.

23. Smith, "Invitation," p. 745.

24. Frank T. Marzials, "Taine's Revolution," *London Quarterly Review* 66 (April 1886), pp. 24–48.

25. A.V. Dicey, "Taine's Gouvernement Revolutionnaire," *The Nation* 40, (26 February 1885), pp. 184–185.

26. Dicey, "Taine's Origins" pp. 274–276.

27. "M. Taine on the Jacobin Conquest," *The Spectator* 55, (18 February 1882), pp. 232–234; *The Nation* 40, 5 March 1885, pp. 206–207.

28. Acton, *Lectures on the French Revolution*, pp. 345–373.

29. Hubert Bourgin, *De Jaurès à Leon Blum: L'École Normale et la politique* (Paris, 1938), p. 271.

30. Alphonse Aulard, *Histoire politique de la Révolution française*, 3d ed. (Paris, 1905), p. 46.

31. This is mainly based on the index to books reviewed by the *Times Literary Supplement* since 1902, the subject indexes of the British Museum (now British Library) since 1881, and the indexes to research libraries in the area of Los Angeles.

32. The subject indexes are for 1881–1900, and thereafter by five-year periods. I have not thought it worth while to break down the first volume further. The estimate is based on a rough column count of the titles listed under the general heading "*France, History, Revolution, Consulate and Empire 1789–1815*", calculating each column as twenty-five titles before 1950, and twenty after. The titles dealing with Napoleon and military history—they usually form the largest part of the list—have been omitted, since it may be assumed that they appeal to a readership with different interests.

33. In the British Museum he scored eleven titles from 1881 to 1900 (in all languages) or one every other year, fourteen from 1901 to 1910, or 1.4 per year. Between the wars he scored nine titles, or less than one every two years.

34. Two of the four titles on him added since the war are in Russian. His writings were translated into Russian in 1923 and 1956 (*Great Soviet Encyclopedia*, English edition, art: Marat). I. Stepanov's *J.P. Marat and His Struggle against Counter-Revolution* had gone through six editions by 1924. Victor Daline, "Lénine et le Jacobinisme," *Annales Historiques de la Révolution Française* 43 (1971): 92.

35. Jacques Godechot, *Un Jury pour la Révolution* (Paris, 1974), p. 319.

36. *Collected Works*, vol. 26, pp. 132, 180–181. Lenin's praise for Danton is particularly significant, since he uses him to impress on his comrades the necessity for the October Revolution and how to conduct such an insurrection.

37. Ernest Labrousse, *La Crise de l'économie française à la fin de l'Ancien Régime et au début de la Révolution* (Paris, 1944); "Comment naissent les révolutions" in *Actes du Centenaire de 1848* (Paris, 1948).

38. Emmanuel Le Roy Ladurie, *Paris-Montpellier:P.C.-P.S.U. 1945–1963* (Paris, 1982).

39. P.M. Jacobs, *History Theses 1901–1970* (London, 1976).

40. *Hommages à la Révolution* (Paris, 1939); *Lyon N'est Plus* 4 vols. (Paris, 1937).

41. Albert Mathiez, *La vie chère et le mouvement social sous la Terreur* (Paris, 1927); Georges Lefebvre, *Les paysans du Nord pendant la Révolution Française* (Paris, 1924); Albert Soboul, *Les sansculottes parisiens en l'an II. Mouvement populaire et gouvernement révolutionnaire* (Paris, 1958).

42. For a convenient guide to the historians of the French Revolution, see Samuel F. Scott and Barry Rothaus, eds. *Historical Dictionary of the French*

Revolution 1789–99, 2 vols. (Westport, 1985), and—more briefly—the *Blackwell Dictionary of Historians* (Oxford, 1987), but not François Furet, "Histoire Universitaire de la Révolution," in François Furet and Mona Ozouf. eds., *Dictionnaire Critique de la Révolution Française* (Paris, 1988), which is best regarded as a personal polemic, in many cases by omission.

43. *Enciclopedia Italiana*, vol. 14, s.v. "Fascismo," p. 847.

44. See Antoine Prost, *Vocabulaire des Proclamations Electorales de 1881, 1885 et 1889* (Paris, 1974), pp. 52–53, 65.

45. "Types of Capitalism in Eighteenth Century France," *English Historical Review* 79 (1964): 478–497 "Non-Capitalist Wealth and the Origins of the French Revolution," *American Historical Review* 79 (1967): 469–496. Art, "Bourgeoisie" in Scott and Rothaus, eds., *Historical Dictionary*.

Chapter 4: Surviving Revision

1. John McManners in *New Cambridge Modern History* vol. 8 (Cambridge, 1965), p. 651. For Crane Brinton's review, *History and Theory* 5 (1966): 315–320.

2. Norman Hampson, "The Two French Revolutions," *New York Review of Books* (13 April 1989), pp. 11–12: Solé, *La révolution en questions*, p. 15.

3. Ibid.

4. "Il faut enfin céder à la nécessité qui nous entraine, il faut ne plus méconnaitre la marche de la société," in *De la force du gouvernement actuel et de la nécessité de s'y rallier*, a defence of the Directory. Cited in M. Gauchet, "Benjamin Constant" in Furet and Ozouf. *Dictionnaire Critique de la Révolution Française* (Paris, 1988), p. 954.

5. Runciman, "Unnecessary Revolution: The Case of France" *European Journal of Sociology* 23 (1982): 318.

6. Solé, *La révolution en questions* pp. 366–367, 372–373, 386–387. Solé specifically acknowledges that "le deferlement des enquêtes et des hypothèses qui a suivi, outre-Manche et outre-Atlantique, depuis une vingtaine d'années, a contribué à renouveler de fond en comble notre compréhension des évènements survenus en France entre 1787 et 1799," p. 13.

7. The fullest statement of Cobban's views in his *The Social Interpretation of the French Revolution* (London, 1964); for his original attack, see *The Myth of the French Revolution* (London, 1955).

8. Runciman, "Unnecessary Revolution," see especially pp. 295, 299, 301.

9. Furet, "Le catechisme révolutionnaire" *Annales E.S.C.*, 24 (1971): 261.

10. Georges Lefebvre, *Études sur la Révolution Française*, 1963; Paris, 1954, pp. 340–341. The text was written in 1932. For instance:

However, as Jaurès presented it, 1789 appeared to be an event both single and simple: the cause of the Revolution was the power of the bourgeoisie which had grown to maturity, and its result was to provide the legal consecration of that power. Today this view strikes us as excessively summary. In the first place, it does not explain why the advent of the bourgeoisie occurred at that moment and not at some other time, and, more particularly, why in France it took the form of a sudden mutation, whereas it could well have taken the form of a gradual, if not an entirely peaceful, evolution, as occurred elsewhere. We now know that for the Revolution, as a specific event to occur in 1789, there had to be a truly extraordinary and unpredictable combination of immediate causes: an exceptionally serious financial crisis, due to the American war; a crisis of unemployment, due to the commercial treaty of 1786 and the Eastern War; and finally, a food and cost-of-living crisis due to the poor harvest of 1788 and the Edict of 1787 which authorized cereal exports and therefore emptied the granaries. But, more than this, the long-term causes of the Revolution themselves now seem increasingly complex to us. It has been demonstrated that the reason why the monarchy could not manage its financial crisis was that its own authority was collapsing. As Mathiez has told us, the king was no longer in a position to govern. [Other authors] ... had already shown that the immediate cause of the Revolution lay in the refusal of the privileged themselves to make the sacrifices which royal power attempted to impose on them, thus extorting from the monarchy the calling of the States-General.... Initially, the revolution was thus not bourgeois but aristocratic ...

It is thus clear that the economic interpretation of history does not commit us to simple views. The rise of a revolutionary class is not necessarily the only cause of its triumph, and it is not *inevitable* that it should be victorious or, in any case, victorious in a violent manner. In the present case the Revolution was launched by those whom it was going to sweep away, not by those who were to be its beneficiaries. Nor can one prove that the aristocrats would necessarily succeed in imposing their will on the sovereign. Nobody can argue that great kings in the 18th century might not have checked the advances of the nobility. Is it impossible to suppose that in 1787, even in 1789, a great king, enjoying high prestige, might have made the nobility see reason? No, it is not."

11. Solé, *La Révolution*, p. 267. "The Marxist myth which sees the

Revolution as a decisive stage in the development of the capitalist economy, is easily refuted by the stagnation of the economy during the revolutionary era and beyond."

12. For example, the introduction to the English edition of "Socialism, Utopian and Scientific" in *Werke*, vol. 22, p. 304.

13. Lefebvre, "La Révolution française et les paysans" in *Etudes* (1963); Albert Soboul, *Précis d'histoire de la Révolution française* (Paris, 1962), p. 477.

14. Lefebvre, "La Révolution," p. 340.

15. R.R. Palmer, *The Age of Democratic Revolution: A Political History of Europe and America 1760–1800*, 2 vols. (Princeton, 1964). Jacques Godechot and R.R. Palmer, "Le problème de l'Atlantique du 17 ème au 20 siècle, International Congress of Historical Sciences, *Relazioni*, vol. 5 (Florence, 1955), pp. 173–240. For the debate, see International Congress, *Atti del 10 Congresso Internazionale* (Rome, 1957), pp. 565–579.

16. R.R. Palmer's sympathetic study of the Committee of Public Safety, *Twelve Who Ruled* (Princeton, 1941), and Jacques Godechot's election to the presidency of the Société des Etudes Robespierristes, would suggest as much.

17. Sir Charles Webster—perhaps the most distinguished historian of international policy in the British official establishment of the time: "The Atlantic was not suggested as a 'region' until the Second World War. The rapporteurs had failed to emphasize sufficiently the unity of the world. For this reason the Atlantic Community might be a temporary phenomenon. It was created by the policy of the USSR and if this changed it might change also." *Atti del 10 Congresso*, p. 571–572.

18. *Ancien Régime* 1:72. Cf. Kahan "Tocqueville's Two Revolutions", pp. 587–588.

19. *Mémoires*, vol. 1, pp. 157–159, cited in the Introduction (by Pierre Rosanvallon) to Guizot, *Histoire de la Civilisation en Europe*, p. 14.

20. Cited in Mellon, *The Political Uses of History*, p. 29.

21. For an extreme statement see Sédillot, *Le coût de la Révolution française*, pp. 268–279.

22. See the entertaining Hervé Hamon and Patrick Rotman, *Les intellocrates: Expédition en haute intelligentsia* (Paris, 1981). It is perhaps not without significance that the list of the twenty-five intellectuals "who play a preponderant role in the circulation of ideas," contains only one person who has written extensively on the French Revolution, namely François Furet; although almost one third of the group is comprised of historians or has historical qualifications.

23. "Pendant trente années les modes idéologiques parisiennes s'accompagnèrent à chaque fois d'une réinterprétation du marxisme" (Raymond Aron. *Memoires* [Paris, 1983], p. 579).

24. Ladurie, *Paris-Montpellier*, pp. 44–45.

25. Tony Judt, *Marxism and the French Left* (Oxford, 1986), p. 183.

26. Ibid., p. 177: "The symbolic moments of revolutionary experience of 1789–1794, and to a lesser extent 1848 and 1871, have entered the vocabulary of all academic thinkers as intellectual reference points. Not only do most French writers over thirty owe their understanding of their political environment to the diffused work of these scholars (Mathiez, Georges Lefebvre, Albert Soboul, as well as Jaurès and Lucien Herr), but it is to Mathiez *et al.* that French intellectuals are perforce obliged to look when seeking an empirical skeleton on which to graft their fleshy metaphysical corpus of thought. It is the French Revolution, understood as a process with meaning, which explains in the last instance all the unresolved contingents in French political reality."

27. Ph. Buonarroti, *Conspiration pour l'égalité dite de Babeuf,* 2 vols. (Brussels, 1828). See Samuel Bernstein, *Buonarroti* (Paris, 1949).

28. See Elisabeth Eisenstein, *The First Professional Revolutionist: Filippo Michele Buonarroti* (Cambridge, 1959).

29. Régis Debray, *Que Vive La République* (Paris, 1989), p. 48: a splendid philippic against those embarrassed by having to celebrate the bicentenary of the Revolution, written with venom and brio. Giraudoux, a highly mannered and sophisticated wit, novelist, and dramatist, much appreciated before 1939, but neglected since 1945 (because of his unsatisfactory political stance), has at last deservedly made it into the *Pléiade* collection of French classics.

30. Godechot, *Un Jury pour la Révolution* (Paris, 1974), p. 324.

31. Pierre Bourdieu, *La Noblesse d'État: Grandes écoles et esprit de corps* (Paris, 1989), p. 296.

32. Brinton, p. 317.

33. J.L. Talmon, *The Origins of Totalitarian Democracy* (London, 1952).

34. The most important Western group of non-Stalinist Marxist intellectuals, the New York Trotskyite community, was already disintegrating, several of its prominent members or ex-members moving in directions that were taking them well outside the Left, although not yet into militant conservatism.

35. For a bibliography of this debate see Perry Anderson. "The Figures of Descent," *New Left Review* 161 (1987): 21n., which is a late 1980s contribution to it. See also Tom Nairn, *The Enchanted Glass: Britain and Its Monarchy* (London, 1988) especially p. 378ff., and the review of that book by A. Arblaster in *New Left Review* 174 (1989): 97–110.

36. For a survey of this debate by a British Germanist, see Richard Evans, "The Myth of Germany's Missing Revolution," *New Left Review* 149 (Jan.-Feb., 1986): 67–94.

37. Arno Mayer, *The Persistence of the Old Regime: Europe to the Great War* (New York, 1981). Cf. David Cannadine's: "Many historians no longer believe that the 19th century saw the middle classes triumph.... There is no reason to explain ... why bourgeois civilisation ultimately collapsed.... It had never actually conquered in the first place." Review of E.J. Hobsbawm, *The Age of Empire* in *New Society*, 23 October 1987, p. 27.

38. William Rubinstein, "The Victorian Middle Classes: Wealth Occupation and Geography" *Economic History Review* 30 (1977): 602–623 and other similar studies by the same author.

39. For the most ambitious project in this field, see J. Kocka ed. *Bürgerlichkeit im 19, Jahrhundert, Deutschland im europäischen Vergleich*, 3 vols. (Munich, 1988).

40. Professor Norman Stone in *The Sunday Times*, 6 March 1988, cited in E.J. Hobsbawm, *Politics for a Rational Left* (London, 1989), p. 224. More generally: James Raven, "British History and the Enterprise Culture" *Past and Present* 123 (May, 1989): 178–204, especially 190–191.

41. See "The Nation State in the Middle East" in Sami Zubaida, *Islam, the People and the State: Essays on Political Ideas and Movements in the Middle East* (London and New York, 1988), especially p. 173.

42. As in the first sentence of the conclusion of Solé, *La Révolution*, p. 337: "Tocqueville et Taine ont vu à juste titre dans la centralisation napoléonienne, le principal résultat de la Révolution." To reduce the effect of a major event in world history to the acceleration of a trend in French state administration, is analogous to saying that the main historic consequence of the Roman Empire was to provide the Catholic Church with a language for Papal Encyclicals.

43. D.G.M. Sutherland, *France 1789–1815: Revolution and Counterrevolution* (London, 1986), p. 49. The differences between this revisionist Canadian historian and the French historian (Solé, *La Révolution*), who often does little more than paraphrase him (compare Sutherland p. 49 and Solé p. 83) is instructive. The one has no trouble in seeing that what is important about "The Revolution of the People" is its revolutionary effect; the other, who adds a question mark after the title of his corresponding chapter, and pays far less attention to the crucial point that the soldiers ceased to be loyal, stresses above all how similar the popular movements of 1789 were to earlier popular protests in past centuries. This is precisely to miss their point: which is not their structure but—in the summer of 1789, or in Russia in February 1917—their *impact*.

44. Rose, *A Century of Continental History*, p. 1.

45. *Collected Letters of Thomas and Jane Welsh Carlyle*, ed. C.R. Sanders and K.J. Fielding (Durham, N.C., 1970–81), vol. 4, p. 446.

46. Rose, *A Century of Continental History*, p. 1.

Index

Echoes of the Marseillaise